An UnOrdinary Life

Anthony Rosen

By the same author

England's Pleasant Land – vision and reality
Farming and the Nation
The Reform of the Common Agricultural Policy
Is there a Life after Subsidies?

**Anthony Rosen asserts the moral right
to be identified as the author of this book**

ISBN 978-1-904499-14-5

Further copies of this book may be obtained from:
www.amazon.co.uk, www.roundtuitpublishing.co.uk or by post from
Roundtuit at the address below

First published in United Kingdom of Great Britain in 2006 by
Roundtuit Publishing, 32 Cookes Wood, Broompark, Durham DH7 7RL

Printed in the United Kingdom of Great Britain by Prontaprint, Durham, 0191 384 3220

These memoirs are dedicated
to my patient and loving wife and family,
my many good friends and my loyal colleagues,
without whom my life would have been
considerably less exciting and far less enjoyable.

FOREWORD

If all of us who lived within the farming industry in the second half of the twentieth century had been asked to nominate the most colourful, John Buchanesque character in our midst, who could it be other than Anthony Rosen?

Farmer, but also army pilot, ocean racer, farming innovator, chairman and board member - and agent provocateur when necessary - of our agricultural institutions, as well as land companies from Britain to California and, notably, to New Zealand. An adviser to many governments including Iran and Algeria, while finding time to be a professional journalist - he is a brilliant stitcher of words - and latterly as leader of farmers' groups to see the world.

His name will always be associated with Fountain Farming, a massive tenant farming company, the biggest in Europe, which grew to 30,000 acres of mixed farming including 5,200 dairy cows and 16,000 acres of cereals and vegetables. All ended in a confused and capricious switching of capital within the Square Mile. But this project, criticised of course by the traditionalists, was an inspired milestone in our farming history and a signpost to a rapidly developing future age.

How did one man undertake this immense range of activity?

His wife, Hilary, provides two chapters of great charm, and hints at having to deal with tireless exuberance in her household. In what seems a delightful understatement, she tells us that 'life was never dull'.

How would Anthony Rosen wish to be remembered by the industry he so nobly served? Without doubt, 'That he always stuck up for agriculture'.

Personal memoirs can be a trifle heavy-on-the-wing. Not so here. This is a 'thumping good read'.

Derek Barber   11th November 2006

(Lord Barber of Tewkesbury)

CONTENTS

IN THE BEGINNING...

There will always be a debate as to how much one is influenced by breeding and how much by one's environment. Certainly my *breeding* provided maximum hybrid vigour but only a remote agricultural bias since my maternal grandfather retired from farming just after the First World War. As for *environment* it must have been the many happy times which I spent on my uncle's farm that provided some subliminal agricultural influence which affected my entire career.

My mother came from good British yeoman stock. Her father, George Bryant, an East Anglian farm manager, married my grandmother, Marion Boddon, a Scots girl, as his second wife (his first having died young) and in 1908 they produced my mother, Phyllis Christine Bryant, in Suffolk. George Bryant was renowned for his strength and competence - a stern but kind man he lives in my memory as a formidable disciplinarian.

After local schooling my mother went on to become an English and music teacher and was, as photographs show, a remarkably beautiful woman. She was also a very good tennis player and it was at the age of nineteen that she met my father at the local tennis club. They fell in love and married within weeks and produced three boys in rapid succession - Michael in 1928, Brian in 1929 and me in 1930, sixteen months between each of us.

In 1933, presumably because she was run-down after producing three children so quickly, she caught the dreaded scourge of the time, tuberculosis. At first the prognosis was good but this was soon to be proved false and, after a year in a sanatorium, she died aged 27, leaving my father in 1936, a widower with three sons, aged eight, six and five.

My father? He was born in Odessa 3rd December 1895, one of twelve children, the son of a highly regarded tea taster and the grandson of the chief rabbi of Kiev in the Ukraine. He was

1

educated at Odessa High School until the anti-Semitic pogroms became more violent. At the start of the 20th century these attacks were mainly carried out by Cossack soldiers who were employed by the Tsars to instil fear throughout Russia. Indeed my father was quite proud of a scar across his back inflicted when he was ten years old by a Cossack with a leaded knout.

As the intensity of the attacks built up and, since my grandfather was offered a good position with a London firm of tea blenders, the family decided to leave Russia and settle in England.

The vanguard were my grandfather, Solomon Rosen, and my father Maurice, aged 14, who, after a week of travel, arrived on Monday 8th August 1910 in Fournier Street, in London's East End, a convenient base for my grandfather's job in the City.

They were welcomed by the locals, both British and fellow expatriates, and liking what they saw, early the next year, leaving my father earning his keep in London working with the tea company, my grandfather Solomon returned to Odessa to collect the remainder of his large family. In 1911 the rest of the family, but without the eldest daughter who had married a Russian diplomat, arrived in England.

The daughter, my aunt Ida, who remained in Russia, produced two sons, both of whom died as lieutenants serving in the Red Army defending Stalingrad – my Russian cousins. Soon after the First World War Aunt Ida and her husband came to London with the Russian Trade delegation. Their stay was relatively short lived for the Delegation was expelled when in October 1924 the MI5 intercepted a letter written by Grigory Zinoviev, chairman of the Comintern in the Soviet Union. In the letter Zinoviev urged British communists to promote revolution through acts of sedition. Vernon Kell, head of MI5 and Sir Basil Thomson head of Special Branch, were convinced that the letter was genuine. Kell showed the letter to Ramsay MacDonald, the Labour Prime Minister. It was agreed that the letter should be kept secret but someone leaked news of the letter to the *Times* and the *Daily Mail*. The letter was published in these newspapers four days before the 1924 General Election and contributed to the defeat of MacDonald and the Labour Party. After the election it was claimed that two of MI5's agents, Sidney Reilly and Arthur Maundy Gregory, had forged the letter and that Major Joseph Ball, a MI5 agent, leaked it to the press. In 1927 Ball went to work for the Conservative Central Office where he pioneered the idea of spin-doctoring. Research carried out by Gill Bennett in 1999 suggested that there were several MI5 and MI6 officers attempting to bring down the Labour Government in 1924, including Stewart Menzies, the future head of MI6.

As a foreign national my father was rejected for military service in the First World War, so he joined the British Red Cross Society as a stretcher bearer. At 22 years of age he was promoted to Commandant of the 314th BRCS Detachment and concurrently Commandant of the 63rd Shoreditch Detachment.

He was a fervent fund raiser then - and for the rest of his life. During the First War he raised sufficient funds to buy his detachment an ambulance, also another ambulance for another detachment and then gave the considerable surplus to London Hospital, for which he was made a Life Governor: he was similarly honoured by St Dunstan's Hostel for the Blind for his fund-raising efforts. According to the detailed records still retained at Kew he was responsible for raising many thousands of pounds and as a result he attended the first post-war Buckingham Palace Garden Party on the 25th July 1919.

When he applied for British naturalisation in 1920 it was bad timing for, to quote the records, "Russian nationals should not be accepted (for naturalisation) except in particular circumstances". The handwritten notes in the margin of his application state: "….the man has done what he could for the country, he might have his certificate", signed Sir J.Pedder. Having duly paid the fee of £9 my father became a proud British citizen on 21st January

3

1921 and spent the rest of his life, fifty years exactly, living up to his beliefs and ever grateful to the country which gave him and his family sanctuary when they needed it.

So it was that six years later he met my mother and they married. Sadly for all too short a time.

Since my mother had spent virtually the whole of the last two years of her life ill at home and later in hospitals, my memories of her are, sadly, very hazy. Dim memories, some presumably stimulated by photographs, of a caring mother who devoted herself to her children and recollections of holidays spent in very comfortable rented cottages in both Walton-on-the-Naze and Canvey Island.

The former stands out for its quiet ambiance and sandy beach: the latter remembered as, even then, a frenetic holiday resort where a distinct memory is of a spectacular diving exhibition where a man dived from a platform sixty feet high in to a tank of water only six feet deep. I recall holding my mother's hand when, as if this dive wasn't spectacular enough, the surface of the water was set on fire. Other memories of my mother are of her confined to hospital and desperate to get better to be with her family again: never complaining, always cheerful when we were with her. But it was not to be and, just as she was due to be transferred to a sanatorium at Hastings for convalescence, she died.

My eight year old brother Michael, even at such a young age, instinctively accepted responsibility for his two younger siblings. This continued throughout our school lives and certainly softened the blow of my mother's death for Brian and me.

One especial memory of my childhood was watching, with my father and two brothers, the Silver Jubilee parade of King George V and Queen Mary in May 1935, from the third floor window of his St Paul's Churchyard office. It was an amazingly hot day and I was fascinated by the number of spectators who fainted, to be

4

rapidly taken away by St John's Ambulance volunteers. There was no overt security and the monarchs' open carriage passed immediately beneath our open window.

After my mother had died we had a very strange existence, moving from pillar to post: many relatives were very kind but three spirited boys were a real handful for anyone to take on. Both my mother's parents and her adopted sister, Stella Payne, tried their best but Stella had three young children of her own to keep her occupied. My grandfather, George Bryant, was a tall fit man but already in his eighties when I first recall him: he had won local fame for plugging the seawall in Canvey Island with farmyard manure when managing a farm on the island. As a younger man having missed the train at Laxfield he ran along the line and caught it at the next stop. Similarly his age did not stop him in 1938 from digging a Morrison air-raid shelter in their garden at Greys, which was only removed in 2003. This bungalow had been built by my uncle George Payne and sold at that time for £250. In 2000 Hilary and I called in on today's owners who were very pleased to have recently bought the property for "only £82,000!"

Thus we three boys had no really settled home life until 1938 when my father bought a house in Saltdean, Sussex, which was handy for his newly established business of manufacturing and retailing suedes, leathers and furs in Hove, just seven miles along the coast.

The peaceful calm of Saltdean, mainly inhabited by retirees, was shattered by the arrival of the three of us. A succession of housekeepers came and went: we were the tearaways of the times, aged 8, 9 and 10, soon joined by a local gang of eager followers. I like to think that we were not actually bad, just high spirited? I wonder though if the builders of the Saltdean Lido ever realised why it took them so long to build this monument to neo-classicism?......

There was a field at Saltdean alongside the main coastal road which made an ideal playground for "our gang". But one day the field was fenced and large "Keep Out" notices appeared, together with the paraphernalia of a massive building site being prepared for the construction of one of the first Lidos, basically a very large swimming pool. Although we welcomed the thought of a pool, in the short term we bitterly resented the fact that we had lost our playground.

Every evening, after the builders had departed, we very carefully dismantled half the brickwork which they had built during the day, cleaning the bricks thoroughly and replacing them in their orderly piles. This went on for weeks and as far as I know nobody knew why the building was not completed by the time the war started.

It was normal for the whole gang to use the steeply sloping verges of the main coastal road, which ran from Brighton to Newhaven, as a cresta run, using both dustbin and breadbin lids or wooden planks as our sleds. Although there were many fewer cars in those days the number of near misses we had were, in retrospect, truly frightening, probably more so for the horrified drivers, stunned as a small boy (there were no girls in our gang) zipped across the road in front of them perched on a breadbin lid.

I think that the final indiscretion for us was the occasion when we found an abandoned motor-cycle and sidecar. It took the gang (the current housekeeper's son, three village youngsters and us three) a week to move it slowly but surely to the top of a very steep hill on the edge of the village. The intention was, once we reached the summit, to climb aboard and Michael would steer us safely to the bottom, down a chalk track about one hundred feet high and one hundred yards long – a gradient of one in three. Fortunately, at least as far as the gang were concerned, but perhaps not for the local residents, as we were arguing as to who should sit where my father appeared and disaster was averted.

Thus it was that once again the three of us were spread around various longsuffering relatives, since obviously we were beyond the control of the well meaning succession of housekeepers. This strange existence continued until outside circumstances were to decide our future – the Second World War.

We were all issued with identity cards, with special additions which entitled us to enter the Coastal Defence Area and then the exciting fitting of our gas masks, each neatly packed in a cardboard box. From the outbreak of war these were supposed to be carried by us everywhere.

My father was extremely worried about his ability to look after us should the Nazis invade Britain as was believed would soon happen. Thus during the phony peace, following Chamberlain's wretched Munich meeting with Hitler in 1938, which promised "peace in our time", my father put our names down to be evacuated to Canada and we were allocated places to go on the second liner, which was due to sail in October 1939.

Tragically, on the 3 September, within hours of Neville Chamberlain declaring war on Germany (Poland having been invaded) a liner , the *Athenia,* carrying some 1,103 civilians from Liverpool to Canada, was torpedoed just west of Scotland. Fortunately the three destroyers, *Electra, Escort* and *Fame,* and two freighters, *City of Flint* and *Southern Cross,* were escorting the *Athenia* and were able to rescue most of those aboard, but still 118 civilians were drowned.

Coincidentally Hilary (my wife to be) and her two brothers had been allocated places on the ill-fated *Athenia* until, shortly before sailing, it was realized that her elder brother, Geoff, was a few months too old to qualify for evacuation, and so they were all taken off the list - all or none.

My father withdrew our names from the Canadian evacuation list, as did many other parents, and instead we were sent to Framlingham College in Suffolk, chosen mainly because we had the amazingly tolerant and hospitable uncle George and aunt Stella (my mother's adopted sister) who farmed only eight miles from the school. In the meantime we had moved into a flat above my father's shop in Hove and my newly widowed maternal grandmother, Marion Bryant, moved in to look after us. We attended Brighton Grammar, the local school.

Neville Chamberlain announced at 11.00am on Sunday 3rd September 1939: *"This morning the British Ambassador in Berlin handed the German Government a final note stating that unless we heard from them by 11 o'clock that they were prepared to withdraw their troops from Poland, a state of war would exist between us. I have to tell you that no such undertaking has been received and that we are at war with Germany"*. At that time France, Australia and New Zealand immediately also declared war on Germany.

We children had imagined, as I believe did many adults, that the moment war was declared there would be an aerial onslaught on Britain by Nazis bombers, probably backed up by invading paratroop landings. It was therefore with considerable trepidation that, as Chamberlain finished his speech on the wireless at 11.15am, we heard the air raid sirens sounding the wailing alarm for the first time. As we watched out of the window, Hove's Western Road cleared as if by magic as people disappeared into the nearest air raid shelter just three doors from us, in the basement below an optician's shop. Before we could go there ourselves the all-clear sounded. It was a false alarm - a private flyer returning to Britain from France.

In 1940 the German armies quickly marched through Belgium and France driving our forces back to the Channel port of Dunkirk where a truly historic rescue in June brought back more than 300,000 fighting men from disaster, albeit most of them without their equipment. The bravest men of all were those who were delegated to be the rear-guard, to remain until they were wounded , killed or captured, thus allowing an amazing number of Allied troops to escape (one of these heroes, Laurie Gould, was much later to become a close friend).

At the time the evacuation from Dunkirk was hailed as a victory especially, as the French immediately surrendered.

It was expected that the Germans would follow across the Channel but they were foiled as they could not control the air space, thanks to the amazing performance of the Royal Air Force.

Indeed the expected Nazi aerial blitzkrieg, as happened to many cities on mainland Europe, took nearly a year to arrive in Britain. It was on the 10 July 1940 that the first massed Luftwaffe raids began what was to be later called the Battle of Britain.

On the 10th May 1940 Chamberlain resigned and Winston Churchill became Prime Minister, much to everyone's relief. At last we had a leader whose charisma inspired everyone - his speeches were bravura performances. We were all glued to our wireless sets when, towards the end of the Battle of Britain, he broadcast to the nation, *Never in the field of human conflict was so much owed by so many to so few. All hearts go out to the fighter pilots, whose brilliant actions we see with our own eyes day after day but we must never forget that all the time, night after night, month after month, our bomber squadrons travel far into Germany, find their targets in the darkness by the highest navigational skill, aims their attacks, often under the heaviest fire, often at serious loss, with deliberate, careful precision, and inflict shattering blows upon the whole of the technical and war-making structure of the Nazi power.*

There were many memorable exploits which we also celebrated. For example there was great excitement when Captain (later Admiral Sir) Philip S. Vian, commanding the destroyer *HMS Cossack,* boarded the German supply ship *Altmark* in Norway on the night of 16th February 1940, rescuing 300 British merchant seaman who had been captured from ships sunk by the German battleship *Graf Spee.* After a hand-to-hand fight with fixed

9

bayonets, the British sailors released the imprisoned seamen and brought them home in triumph.

During the Battle of Britain, from the first German mass air raid until 31 October 1940, some 2,353 British fighter pilots and 574 from overseas took part in the epic air struggle to maintain Britain's freedom. It is difficult to conceive the stress and dangers on the pilots resulting from as many as five battle sorties in one day. Sadly 544 of these pilots were killed during the battle and a further 791 of them died later in the war.

Throughout the summer holidays – and the weather was hot and sunny every day, or so it seemed - we used to cycle the few miles from Hove to the South Downs and watch the dogfights in the sky. It was a real aerial pageant. When one of the enemy was shot down we cheered: when one of ours was we booed. At that young age we did not associate the aircraft in the sky with human life. It wasn't till later in the war that one realized the true horror. For young schoolboys it was a thrilling break from school. At that young age we never contemplated for a moment that Britain would not win the war. The fact that the local beaches were now covered in coils of barbed wire, and mined, and much of the seafront was "out of bounds" was simply an inconvenience.

FRAMLINGHAM COLLEGE [1940-1948]

Framlingham College had been founded in Suffolk in 1864 as the Prince Albert Memorial College, in commemoration of Queen Victoria's Consort who had died two years earlier.

The original college prospectus proudly stated in capital letters that: "…..EACH BOY HAS A SEPARATE BED and the dormitories are spacious and airy". Originally there had been room for 250 boarders. In the 1940s the same dormitories were still very spacious and airy: mine, the Stradbrook House dorm contained no fewer than 48 beds and had no form of heating whatsoever: airy indeed.

The college was originally intended for the sons of clergy and of Suffolk folk. It soon became apparent that the annual cost of £25 per pupil was too expensive to be able to fill the school with boys from Suffolk and so this restriction was lifted. When my two brothers and I went there in 1940 there was still a ten percent discount on the fees for those living in Suffolk and another ten per cent discount for brothers.

In 1877 the school had reached its maximum number of pupils for a hundred years, with a total of 325 boys, but by the time we joined in September 1940 school numbers had dropped to 125, of which a third were day boys, mainly due to the war and its generally run down amenities and poor reputation. I was the 5387 pupil since the school was founded. The fees were £100 per annum for boarders and £33 for dayboys, both amounts before discounts.

My elder brother Michael, aged 12, enrolled as a boarder: my brother Brian and I, aged 11 and 9 on the day we started, were initially to be day boys living at Parham with my maternal widowed grandmother, truly one of the greatest positive influences in my life and known to all as "The Good Granny". She had been installed in a rented four bedroomed house, the

11

High House Farmhouse at Parham, a village two miles from the school. The rent was the princely sum of ten shillings (50 pence) a week. Brian and I cycled to school in all weathers.

All three of us were good at games throughout our school lives but I would prefer to draw a veil over our academic achievements which are better forgotten. Slightly in our defence, with the war raging and all the young teachers away serving the country in the forces, Framlingham, like others, was not over endowed with young enthusiastic teachers, most of teachers who were there having been called back from retirement. So different from today when Framlingham College maintains an outstanding academic record and also shines at sports. I remember that the school was given a half-day holiday because one of the brighter boys had gained a credit in School Certificate Latin!

There were many excitements connected with the war. One day I was cycling home close behind a Valentine tank on the main road from Framlingham to Parham: suddenly the tank threw one of its tracks and the flying track cut straight through one of the roadside trees which was about twelve inches in diameter. I learned my lesson and never followed a tank again.

One remembers when General Sir Edmund Ironside inspected the Junior Training Corps but mainly because he seemed so old – probably at least fifty! On 27th May 1940 Churchill had appointed General Ironside as Commander-in-Chief Home Forces, in charge of organising Britain's defenses: firstly with the LDV (Local Defence Volunteers), within a few months to be renamed as the Home Guard. By the end of July one and a half million men had volunteered, a huge figure which reveals the seriousness with which ordinary people took the threat of invasion in the summer of 1940.

At school all the daily newspapers were devoured avidly as everyone, even the youngest boy, was keen to follow the progress of the war. These being in the days before the invention of photocopiers there was a great demand for newspaper cuttings for our personal scrap-books. Generally one could "bag" a particular piece by circling it in the newspaper and writing one's name alongside – then, provided a prefect did not want it, one could cut it out the next day.

On the last day of our first term, December 19th 1940, there was a great deal of excitement at school as two Spitfires endeavoured to shoot down a rogue barrage balloon over the college. It had broken free of its moorings and was causing havoc on the ground as its dragging chains were strong enough to demolish buildings. As the empty cartridge cases rained down on the college from the Spitfires' machine guns the masters tried ineffectively to keep us inside and attempted to prevent us all from collecting these exciting souvenirs: I imagine a brass cartridge case on one's head would have been quite painful, perhaps worse? Luckily there were no casualties and we watched as the balloon floated away in the distance.

Just a few days later, on 30th December, my father took me to the City of London to see if his office in St Paul's Churchyard was still there. It wasn't - the whole city was ablaze as a result of the massive German bombing attack the night before. St Paul's Cathedral stood alone; every other building within three hundred yards had been destroyed in the inferno.

At school there was a continual debate on our military set-backs and our all-too-few victories: we had large maps on the house-room walls with a daily updating of flags depicting the state of battle. The retreat from Dunkirk, which had taken place in May 1940, some four months before we joined the school, was still a hot topic of discussion because the very popular headmaster, W.H.A.Whitworth, a keen yachtsman who had won the Military Cross in the First World War, disappeared for a few days and it was assumed that he had become one of the "small ships" which helped achieve the amazing rescue of more than 300,000 troops from the beaches. Indeed he was asked to leave the school, in

13

December 1940, at the end of my first term, because, it was rumoured, that he had sailed to Dunkirk in defiance of the expressed wishes of the school governors.

The new headmaster RW Kirkman was a far more serious minded individual and was, in hindsight, probably what the school needed to boost numbers and re-instill much needed discipline.

Nearly all the boarders used the so-called *Framlingham Express* which ran from the main line at Wickham Market through half a dozen small villages to Framlingham. It is amazing how quickly a roll of toilet paper unrolls when held on a spindle out of a train window!

If a passenger wanted to alight at one of these platform-less stations they would wave out of the window and the guard would walk down the line with a small set of steps.

Often the driver would have to stop the train at a level crossing, get down and open the gates: having driven through the train would stop again to allow the guard to shut the gates.

Although food was strictly rationed I do not recall ever being hungry, even allowing for the very active lives we all led. Sport was a daily occurrence although we were limited by the distance we could travel to play away matches. Local army and RAF establishments provided formidable sporting opposition throughout the war.

Some of the playing fields were ploughed up to produce food and all boys were expected to volunteer for helping, especially potato and pea picking, even during the school holidays.

Throughout the war the names of the military leaders were familiar to everyone and their exploits were carefully followed. There was much rejoicing when the Nazis invaded Russia on 22nd June 1941 for now it meant that Hitler was fighting on two major fronts.

The USA joined the war effort following the disaster at Pearl Harbour on 7th December 1941, which came as a complete surprise to the Americans. They were not prepared for an attack and with just three waves of Japanese planes three quarters of the American planes stationed in Pearl Harbour were destroyed. All eight battleships in the Harbour were damaged and 2,300 men were killed. President Roosevelt called it a "date which will live in infamy".

The immediate result of America joining our war effort against the Nazi Axis was a massive input into building American air bases, especially throughout East Anglia, including one of their biggest near our previously rented house at Parham. The intention was that the Americans would carry out their missions during daylight while the British would continue with night bombing.

Once the US bombing of Germany was in full swing we would watch in awe as the massive formations of Flying Fortresses flew over the school. The theory behind the design of the American B-17, the Flying Fortress, was that when ten of these aircraft, each crewed by ten men, flew in a tight formation they would be virtually impregnable to enemy fighter attack since there was complete machine gun (0.5 inch) coverage of all angles of attack. Because it was intended that all ten aircraft in the formation would stick together throughout the flight there was only one navigator - in the lead aircraft.

The Americans soon realized that both these ideas were fallacious because enemy anti-aircraft fire and mechanical problems could cause aircraft to lose their place in the tight formation thus opening serious gaps in the defensive pattern. They quickly trained more navigators so that every aircraft carried one, but they could not solve the problem of the vulnerability of the "box" once a stricken aircraft had left a gap in their defences.

Every day there would be at least one crashed bomber within a few miles of the school. These were, rather ghoulishly, a continuing source of souvenirs for us. One day a member of the RAF Special Investigation Branch came to the school and we were all assembled in the dining hall. He explained that they understood our souvenir hunting but it was of great importance that every item that had been "rescued" that day from the crashed B-17 at Saxted Green, three miles from the school, should be returned to the head prefect's study by five o'clock. Long before the deadline the study was crammed full of souvenirs, including a complete 0.5 inch machine gun! But most important of all was the recovery of the top secret Norden bomb sight.

I still have scars on my left thumb and forefinger incurred whilst dismantling a 0.5 inch cartridge case and not letting the six inch nail go quickly enough as the detonator was deliberately exploded. Mischievous boys seemed to lead a charmed life. We soon learned not to dismantle the cannon shells with white tips - these were tracer shells containing phosphorous which ignited on contact with air. With others, though, the cordite released provided innocent bomb making. In fact our leading schoolboy bomb-maker, who shall remain nameless, in later life became a distinguished clergyman.

We all became "temporary" friends with the "Yanks at Par-Ham". "Temporary" because the rate of attrition amongst the air crews was chillingly high. They played us at cricket and we played them at baseball, but all too soon we realized it was better not to ask "Where's Joe today?" when Joe failed to appear. There was also a palpable difference between the new flyers, full of youthful enthusiasm and keenness to bomb the Nazis war machine, and those more experienced flyers who had survived long enough to be approaching twenty five raids and thus due for a non-flying job. It was all too obvious that the stresses on these men were massive, but they all tried to hide it from us.

The Americans introduced us to the delights of peanut butter, which they had brought with them in prodigious quantities. We introduced them to our home produced chocolate spread, made by mixing cocoa powder, which was surprisingly easy to obtain, sugar and water, stirred with a wooden ruler.

There was great sadness when we heard that the son of the US Ambassador, John Winant, a good friend to Britain and a personal friend of Winston Churchill (appointed ambassador following the appalling behaviour of his predecessor, the anti-British criminal Joe Kennedy) was shot down while flying on his first mission from Parham and spent the rest of the war in prison camp in Germany.

In 1942 Brian and I also became boarders and the Good Granny moved to her adopted daughter's, Stella Payne, farmhouse at Huntingfield, nine miles from the college. This was to be, throughout the rest of our school life, a wonderful haven for Sunday lunches and many school holidays. My long-suffering Aunt Stella and Uncle George never complained when we arrived completely unexpectedly from school on our bicycles for Sunday lunch, bringing with us a few extra boys, all grateful for a really lovely farmhouse meal.

In spite of strict food rationing I do not believe that there was any malnutrition: but certainly we all welcomed the lunches at my uncle's farm, the High House at Huntingfield, where various farm animals "died" mysteriously.

It is difficult to reconcile the weekly ration allowances with what is consumed today. These were: bacon/ham, 4 ounces (100 grams): meat, £0.1.2 (6 pence today): cheese, 2 ounces: margarine, 4 ounces: butter, 2 ounces: milk, 3 pints (plus occasional extra dried milk powder): sugar, 8 ounces: jam, 2 ounces: tea, 2 ounces: 1 egg: and 3 ounces of sweets.

The 'National Loaf' was introduced. It was made with more of the grain than was used in white bread, resulting in a brown loaf.

White bread was no longer readily available and brown bread became the norm. Part of the work of the newly created Ministry of Food was to give advice to the British public on how to make the best of the food available. This included radio broadcasts, cookery demonstrations and recipe leaflets. 'Dr Carrot' and 'Potato Pete' were characters introduced to encourage people to eat home grown vegetables which were plentiful. Very occasionally one would find a tiny piece of eggshell in the school scrambled egg dish, proving that at least one whole egg had been added to the vast concoction of dried eggs!

'Woolton Pie', named after Lord Woolton, the Minister of Food was a popular meal. It consisted of mashed potatoes, cauliflower, swede, carrots, marmite, oatmeal, spring onions, grated cheese and gravy. This was only served at school on special occasions.

All schoolchildren had to have a daily dose of cod-liver oil and malt. The fortunate ones managed to obtain this in the form of Virol, a sweet and sticky mixture, much enjoyed if spread on buttered bread. The unfortunates had raw cod-liver oil which was truly sickening. Special arrangements were made for young children, expectant and nursing mothers to receive cod-liver oil, orange juice and milk from welfare clinics. When oranges were available children less than six years of age were entitled to receive 1lb each week. The general health of children improved and on average they were taller and heavier than children before the war and there were no overweight children, or indeed overweight adults. Food rationing did not end until 1954 when finally meat was freed from restrictions.

Little did I know at the time as we listened with horror to the battle for Stalingrad which lasted from 19 August 1942 until 2 February 1943, in which the Germans lost 110,000 killed during the battle and a further 91,000 were made prisoner (of which fewer than 5,000 survived their imprisonment in Russia) that my two oldest first cousins were fighting and dying there as lieutenants in the Red Army.

At Framlingham, about twice a month, the air raid sirens would sound and all the boarders would have to file down to the ground floor corridors where we spent the rest of the night trying to sleep on our bedclothes spread over the stone floor, until the all clear siren. Only one bomb dropped on Framlingham Town - this destroyed the village Primary School killing a teacher.

School holidays were spent either at the farm or at home in Hove, where we had to have special permission to enter the "Coastal Defence Zone". On 19th August 1942 Brian and I took the bus along the seafront from Brighton to visit our old home at Saltdean. The bus ride ended at Rottingdean leaving us to walk the last mile to our former house. We noticed on the bus ride that, overnight, Bofors anti-aircraft guns had appeared every quarter mile along the cliff edge and when passing the small harbour at Rottingdean we saw that it was full of military ambulances and naval boats. For the first time I realized what war really meant as we watched the injured and the dead being brought ashore in the aftermath of the disastrous Dieppe raid. This was the first time the reality of war was made clear to us: war was not only aircraft fighting in the sky but actually involved human beings.

Later, many years later, it was revealed that the troops involved in the raid on Dieppe exceeded 6,000, of whom roughly 5,000 were Canadian, the remainder being British Commandos, together with 50 American Rangers. The raid had been supported by eight Allied destroyers and 74 Allied air squadrons (eight belonging to the RCAF). The raid also produced a tremendous air battle, part of which we could see out at sea. While the Allied air forces were able to provide protection from the Luftwaffe for the ships off Dieppe, the cost was high. The RAF lost 106 aircraft, which was to be the highest single-day total of the war. The RCAF lost 13 aircraft.

Later the view was expressed that the men who perished at Dieppe were instrumental in saving countless lives on D-Day, 6th

June, 1944. While there can be no doubt that valuable military lessons were learned from this raid on Dieppe, an horrendous price was paid. Of the 4,963 Canadians who embarked on the operation only 2,210 returned to England, and many of these were wounded. There were 3,367 casualties, including 1,946 prisoners of war; 907 Canadians lost their lives. It seemed that Brighton and Hove were the main bases for Canadian troops and it was suggested that their too frequent drunken escapades were as a result of their getting bored waiting for action – the Dieppe Raid seemed an extreme solution. Later, as Allied forces massed in the south of England for D-Day, Hove, along with all other towns along the coast, became a massive equipment and tank laager with again a massive Canadian input.

During school Easter holidays in April 1944 a rumour raced around Hove that there was an important meeting taking place in the Town Hall. I, a thirteen year old, along with about fifty other people, rushed to the Town Hall, soon to be rewarded by the appearance on the steps of Prime Minister Winston Churchill, the Supreme Commander Allied Powers in Europe General Dwight Eisenhower (later US President) and Free French leader General de Gaulle: later we realised that they must have been discussing the plans for the D-Day invasion of Normandy. How true were the wartime words of warning that "walls have ears".

As D-Day (6th June 1944) approached more and more tanks, guns and other military equipment moved into the south of England. Nearby Shoreham Harbour was literally full of tank landing craft while every one of the wide avenues in Hove had a row of camouflaged tanks parked down the centre. Had the Germans had an effective aerial reconnaissance they would have been amazed at the instantaneous growth of these avenues of trees.

At school the progress of the war was followed closely, especially as a great many boys who had left school earlier were soon in the middle of the battles, some to return, some sadly to be added to the ever growing list of "In Memoriam". The famous, much decorated, Group Captain Percy Pickard, paid two visits to his old school before he too made the ultimate sacrifice, aged 27, when leading the Mosquito attack on *Operation Jericho* on the Amiens Gestapo jail to free the 750 prisoners, of which many were high-ranking French Resistance fighters: 258 prisoners escaped, 50 of them resistance fighters. Pickard was an inspirational leader and we had all seen the film "Target for Tonight" many times in which Pickard played the pilot of the Wellington bomber "F for Freddy", part of which had been filmed during actual combat. An impressive man, he stood 6' 4" tall and was a great pre-war RAF polo player. He was awarded three DSOs, the only RAF man to do this in one war and the DFC, as well as the Czech Grand Cross.

There were so many old boys who died that one cannot write about them all, but one who will never be forgotten by those who knew and respected him was Head of School in 1942, Glyn Bateman Whittaker: an outstanding scholar and also probably the greatest sportsman the school had ever seen: uniquely he was captain of rugby, hockey, squash, fives and swimming. He, as a lieutenant in the Royal Marine Commandos, was killed in Normandy in 1944 so tragically soon after singing "Roses of Picardy" at his final school concert.

Indeed for a school as relatively small as Framlingham the Roll of Honour was frighteningly long with more than fifty Old Framlinghamians being decorated for valour and nearly one hundred old boys giving their lives in the service of their country. What a tragic waste of life.

Immediately following the D-Day landings in Normandy, the German V-1s, the Doodlebugs, were a menace in Suffolk, especially to those taking examinations which were continually interrupted as the V-1 engines cut out and the flying bombs crashed – luckily none landed too near the school. In London more than 3,000 civilians were killed by the V-1s.

When the V-2 rockets started there was considerable fear because the first one heard of this fearsome rocket was when the one ton warhead exploded: we were fortunate in that the V-2 rockets were never targeted onto the Framlingham area.

Immediately following September 17th 1944 the wirelesses at school were on all day and all the newspapers were scoured for information on Operation Market Garden: this was, we soon learned, the largest airborne-operation in history. It was a battle for the major strategic bridge over the Rhine at Arnhem. We heard that 35,000 paratroopers had been dropped and another 10,000 men had been flown in there by gliders. Ten years later I learnt that one of my flying instructors, Tom Pearce, had been one of only three glider pilots who had been neither killed nor captured at Arnhem. The bridge was taken and held, but only for four days, as it later transpired our intelligence had ignored a Nazi Panzer tank regiment resting near-by. Only 2,400 men returned safely. All the others were dead, injured or taken prisoner. This operation was later called "A bridge too far".

Just before we broke up for our summer holidays in 1944 there was great excitement generated by reports that there had been a bomb plot to assassinate Hitler. We soon heard that Hitler had unfortunately been only slightly injured in spite of his war room being virtually destroyed and four of his compatriots killed in the blast. Later we were to learn of the barbaric reparations taken by Hitler against those he considered implicated in this abortive attempt on his life.

A much decorated and wounded veteran, Major Claus von Stauffenberg, had planted the bomb and then left the building. Over the next few months most of the group, including Admiral Wilhelm Canaris and many other prominent Germans, were either executed or committed suicide. The great German hero of North Africa, Field Marshall (the youngest ever German in that rank) Erwin Rommel, nicknamed the Desert Fox by both allies and enemies, was one of the plotters and was offered the choice

22

of trial or suicide: he chose the latter. It is estimated that 4,980 Germans were executed after the July Plot. Hitler decided that the leaders should have a slow death. They were hung with piano wire from meat-hooks. Their executions were filmed and later shown to senior members of both the Nationalsozialistische Deutsche Arbeiterpartei (NSDAP – the Nazi Party) and the armed forces as an example to others.

The harsh facts of a life at war, especially for Jewish citizens in Nazi occupied countries, were also brought home to us in 1945 when my father accepted responsibility for a sixteen year Czech boy called Josef Perl. Josef had spent four years in German concentration camps, the last two years in Bergen-Belsen, before being liberated on April 15th 1945 by the British army.

It was after the war was over that we learned that Bergen-Belsen was a concentration camp in Germany. Located between the villages of Bergen and Belsen, built in 1940, it was firstly a prisoner-of-war camp for French and Belgium prisoners. In 1941, it was renamed Stalag 311 and housed about 20,000 Russian prisoners. The camp changed its name to Bergen-Belsen and was converted into a concentration camp in 1943. Jews with foreign passports were kept there to be exchanged for German nationals imprisoned abroad, although very few exchanges were made. About 200 Jews were allowed to immigrate to Palestine and about 1,500 Hungarian Jews were allowed to immigrate to Switzerland, both took place under the rubric of exchanges for German nationals. Bergen-Belsen mainly served as a holding camp for the Jewish prisoners.

The camp was divided into eight sections, a detention camp, two women's camps, a special camp, neutrals camps, "star" camp (mainly Dutch prisoners who wore a Star of David on their clothing instead of the camp uniform), Hungarian camp and a tent camp. It was designed to hold 10,000 prisoners. However, by the war's end more than 60,000 prisoners were detained there, due to the large numbers of those evacuated from Auschwitz and other camps from the East. Tens of thousands of prisoners from other camps came to Bergen-Belsen after agonizing death marches. While Bergen-Belsen contained no gas chambers, more than 35,000 people died there of starvation, overwork, disease, brutality and sadistic medical experiments. It was the first major camp to be liberated by the allies, the event received a lot of press coverage and the world saw the horrors of the Holocaust.

Afterwards in the camp, about 500 people died daily of starvation and typhus. Mass graves were made to hold the thousands of corpses of those who perished. In all it is estimated that there were more than 15,000 concentrations camps established by the Nazis. The camp – which I later visited in 1952 – was a truly appalling example of man's inhumanity to fellow man.

On liberation the British troops were horrified to realize that not all the surviving inmates could be saved. They found at least 10,000 unburied corpses and more than 40,000 sick and dying prisoners. Among the living inmates, 28,000 died after liberation. The inmates had been abandoned in Bergen-Belsen by the Germans, left behind to die.

Josef Perl, suffering from TB in his knees, believed that his entire family had been destroyed by the Nazis but two years later it was discovered by the Red Cross that an elder sister had survived and in 1948 Josef went to live with her. Josef would not talk of his time in the camps, except to reveal that during the harsh winter of 1944 he had escaped from Belsen. But deep in the heart of Germany, after three weeks living wild he was so desperately cold and hungry that he broke back into the camp by joining one of the outside work parties. His decision to return to the horrendous camp was incomprehensible to those of us who had not endured those unspeakable conditions prevailing throughout Germany. Josef went on to become a successful hotelier in Bournemouth.

It was only later that one became fully aware of the true enormity of the vileness of the Nazis but until then enough had been known to bring shame on those countries which did nothing to mitigate the situation. Nobody has ever given a legitimate reason for the failure of the Allies to at least bomb the rail lines to the camps?

Soon after the end of the war in Europe, 8th May 1945, the college's Junior Training Corps were marched a mile to the nearby army rifle ranges to fire .303 live ammunition for the first time. When it came to my turn I found that at one hundred yards range I could hardly see the bulls-eye and found it impossible to hold the rifle steady. I pulled the trigger five times in quick succession as the target appeared. Much to everyone's surprise, especially mine, I was the only one to fire a 4 inch group: sadly I was never to repeat this feat: my prize was a large bar of Cadbury's chocolate.

As soon as I reached sixteen years old I passed the test for riding a motor-cycle. Contrary to school rules I kept the bike, a 350cc BSA, KPE II, about one mile from the school in a shed belonging to the local fish-and-chip shop. This was most popular for spins out to local pubs since we could go beyond the reach of the masters' cycles. When even more stringent fuel restrictions were brought in October 1947 I deemed it prudent to take my bike home to Hove. Thursday 20th November 1947 was a national holiday because Princess Elizabeth was marrying Prince Philip. I obtained permission, not from the school but from the police, to ride my motor-bike home. I set out early and rode 170 miles in torrential rain - quite a marathon. Then I caught the train from Brighton to London and back to Framlingham, reaching school just in time for evening roll-call.

On the train I chatted to an army padre who had been one of those incorrigible escapers who had been interred in Colditz Castle. At that time the world knew little of these heroes as their histories were yet to be published.

School was the making of so many boys but I think that it was especially so for the three Rosens since we desperately needed the routine and discipline involved. But, largely because of our sporting capabilities, we all thoroughly enjoyed our time there - and reading a novel a day whilst in the sixth form must have taught me something?

During the 1940s sport was dominant at Framlingham and the school heroes were not the minority who passed exams and went on to university but those who excelled at sport. Of the four senior houses Stradbrooke House (colour Scarlet) had a big advantage of being the only house in which all the forty-eight boys slept in one dormitory, morale was high because even the most junior boys heard the seniors discussing the tactics for the next day's house matches and were thoroughly integrated as part of the "Scarlet Team". I am certain that this was a major contributing factor as to why, at that time, Stradbrooke was dominant in virtually all sports.

Michael turned out to be one of the school's most outstanding rugby players going on to play for the Senior Sussex team while still a teenager. At Framlingham he was captain of rugby, hockey, athletics and tennis and also played cricket for the school. Brian followed in his footsteps, representing the school at rugby (as vice-captain), hockey, cricket and tennis. I captained the rugby and tennis teams and played hockey (as vice-captain) and cricket (occasionally) and fives for the school. All three of us were in Stradbrooke House and during my five years in the House I never played in any House sports team that did not win.

My two brothers and I only twice played together in a rugby team: the first time was in a House Match when Brian had to retire at half-time with a torn knee cartilage. The second time was four years later when playing together for Brighton Technical College (now rather grander being part of Brighton University) Brian went off halfway through the match with a broken leg.

Michael's back was permanently damaged playing rugby, Brian still has a limp and I suffered frequent painful dislocations to my left shoulder until it was operated upon. Later Hilary was to insist, not unreasonably, that our two sons should go to Charterhouse, a non-rugby playing school.

At the end of the winter term in 1946 one of the school leavers broke into the linen-room to enable him to climb the school spire, there to place a metal chamber-pot on the spike. He owned up to breaking into the linen room before anyone in authority saw the chamber-pot and he was summarily expelled. However once the headmaster realised why he had broken into the linen room and saw the funny side, he was reinstated as an Old Boy – a truly Solomonesque decision!

Once I had obtained (just) my Matriculation in July 1946 my academic schooling effectively ended, although I did not leave for another five terms, sport being the incentive for staying on. My final Latin master, a newly demobilised RAF pilot with three DFCs and serious shell-shock, summed up my academic abilities by writing in my report: "Rosen Minimus knows no Latin, has never known any Latin, and has made it quite plain that he never intends to learn any Latin".

We all studied the war maps at school and each decided where the war would end since we imagined that it would only finish when the last defenders were encircled and either surrendered or were wiped out. I choose Nuremberg – perhaps, remembering the War Criminal Trials my choice was correct?

But the jubilation was unbounded when, on 8th May 1945, the European war came to an end and there was no doubt in all our thoughts that Winston Churchill was the true hero. Thus at our innocent age we could not understand how the nation could dispense with his services at the General Election of the following July: a landslide victory for Clement Attlee (who?) and Labour with a majority of 146 over all other parties - this in the middle of the vital Potsdam Conference to finalise the splitting up of the various European nations between East and West.

During the following school holidays I recall with great clarity the radio report of the dropping of the atom bomb on Hiroshima: then an even greater surprise when the Japanese still refused to surrender with the subsequent death of nearly 50,000 inhabitants of Nagasaki after the second bomb.

At the time there was a complete consensus that the dropping of these weapons had saved the lives of millions of people who would have been killed if Japan had fought to the death as they intended. The Atomic Bombs were the face-savers that allowed the Japanese to surrender with minimum loss of face, so important to them.

Churchill had always insisted that there would not have been a Second World War had the British stood up to the aggression of the Nazis in the mid-thirties. On Stanley Baldwin's eightieth birthday in 1947 Churchill declined to send him a message of good wishes. Instead he said: "I wish Stanley Baldwin no ill, but it would have been better for our country if he had never lived".

Then with the war over and the ending of the transatlantic food supplies from America food rationing became tighter, even bread being rationed for the first time in 1947. Coincidentally this was one of the longest and coldest winters on record. The Framlingham Meres (owned by the college) froze over early in January and did not thaw until the middle of March allowing ice skaters, proficient and potential, nearly ten weeks of glorious exercise. There were no field sports until the last ten days of the Spring term but Stradbrooke, during this brief interlude in the bad weather, managed to beat the other three houses at hockey. As a result, creating a rather unusual precedent of awarding school colours although the recipients had not played in a school match, Roy Quinlan and I were awarded 1st Xl hockey colours.

In autumn 1947 somehow clothes rationing rules were loosened and Framlingham bought a set of chocolate and blue (the school colours) rugby vests for the rugby 1st XV: I remember with pride wearing these splendid shirts for the first time on 18th October 1947 when leading the team on to the field to beat HMS Ganges 8 points to 3.

I am always surprised at how little bullying there was at Fram compared with what one reads, or hears, of boys' experiences at other public schools. Throughout my eight years there I can recall only two such offenders (nameless, but numbered 5455 & 5565) – neither has been seen at old-boy functions since they left in 1944 - thank goodness.

As soon as the war ended in August 1945 with the dropping of the second atomic bomb on Nagasaki, my Uncle George brought his 1933 12-metre yacht *Zelita* out of mothballs. George was an amazing sailor having left school aged fourteen and gone to sea in the last of the great Clipper ships, sailing in grain clippers around Cape Horn and the Cape of Good Hope a number of times.

One of his sailing ships, the Copenhagen, went down off Cape Horn with the loss of all hands. It is said still to haunt Cape Horn.

Stella and George's three children, Marion, George and Philip, together with my brother Brian and me, often made up the willing crew of *Zelita* in school holidays and we made many interesting voyages to France, Belgium and Holland, as well as the West Country ports, especially Torbay.

On berthing in Boulogne in April 1947 there had to be an armed gendarme to protect the boat from the French locals who were, to put it mildly, still very anti-British. When one saw the almost total devastation of many French towns (Caen looked as though it had been annihilated, caused especially by our pre-D-Day bombing and shelling) one could almost see why.

Later that year we sailed from Dover to Ostend where a pack of twenty duty-free cigarettes could be bought for eleven old pennies (4½ new pence) and although none of us smoked we bought a few boxes. A few days later we sailed in to Rotterdam, a town flattened by German bombers after the Dutch had surrendered in 1940. The Dutch welcomed us with tremendous enthusiasm as tourists were very much a novelty and there can be no doubt that the Dutch were our closest wartime allies, in spite of the time it took for the Allied forces to evict the Nazi invaders in 1945. Close to the yacht club where *Zelita* was berthed was the (still famous) Old Dutch Restaurant where we decided to dine.

After a truly superb meal, including the first steaks that the five younger crew members had ever eaten, we were about to be presented with the bill. However before giving it to us the Maitre d'Hotel asked us if we had any cigarettes and would we like to pay with them instead of cash? (At that time when one travelled overseas one was allowed to take only £5). We asked how many cigarettes he would like for the meal for the seven of us: "Would a packet be all right, for the seven?" he enquired. We told him we would return for lunch the next day with the cigarettes.

We returned, and when we presented the Maitre d'Hotel with a packet from each of us for our dinners the previous night the red carpet was truly laid out. We ate there six times during our stay and at the final dinner presented them with a carton of 200 cigarettes as a tip. The entire restaurant staff clapped us out. I am still determined that I will return one day.

[Today, 59 years later, the leading guide to Rotterdam dining reports about the Old Dutch: *This atmospheric place, housed in what was once a traditional home is one of the city's most memorable restaurants. It offers traditional Dutch dishes and the best in French cuisine. The wild duck breast in elderberry sauce is an excellent main course; try the walnut parfait drizzled with honey for dessert.*]

When I left school in April 1948 it was to spend the next two and a half years effectively wasting my time, at least academically, at Brighton Technical College, occasionally attending lectures, but actually becoming quite a good tennis player and a most proficient motor cycle racer on a 1948 350cc BSA Gold Star, which I had bought virtually new for £180, say half a year's salary at that time.

In 1948 I did win both the Sussex and Suffolk junior tennis doubles championships and managed to reach the third round of the Wimbledon Junior Doubles. In addition I won the Brighton & Hove Motor Cycle Club's cup for winning the most points for the Club in motor-cycling grass track and scrambling racing. At the same time I was playing hockey for Brighton & Hove and occasionally for the Sussex County team. I had been given student deferment from National Service while I supposedly attended B.Sc. engineering classes.

Brother Brian and I attended virtually all the events at the 1948 London Olympics which started on the 29th July at Wembley Stadium, staying at our medical student cousin Ivor Rosen's flat in Maida Vale. My three major memories were the amazing performances of Dutchwoman Fanny Blankers-Koen. She won the 100 metres, 200 metres and the 80 metres hurdles in addition to being the anchor leg on the winning Dutch relay team. She was deprived of more titles by a rule limiting women to three individual events in track and field athletics, at a time when she was also the world record holder in the high jump and long jump.

Another memory was of that great sportsman from Czechoslovakia, Emil Zátopek, who began his illustrious Olympic career at these games by running the 10,000 metres in which he took the lead during the tenth of 25 laps. Eventually he lapped all but two runners and won by more than 300 metres. Only three days later, Zátopek ran in the final of the 5,000 metres. At the start of the final lap, he trailed Gaston Reiff of Belgium by 50 metres and Zátopek thrilled everyone with a sprint which pulled him closer and closer, but Reiff noticed Zátopek and pulled out a magnificent spurt just in time and won by 1½ metres.

But the greatest excitement of all for my brother and me was Old Framlinghamian Norman Borrett's captaining of the British hockey team which swept through the tournament, only to lose in the final to India by 4 goals to none, providing the victors with their first ever Olympic gold medal.

Looking back I wish that I had made more of my (not completely lacking?) scholastic abilities. I excuse myself, half-heartedly, in that there was definitely a lack of motivation and encouragement at that time.

My mother, Phyllis Rosen, died 1936, aged 27

Anthony, Brian and Michael – the age of innocence

The Good Granny,
Marion Bryant,
died 1953,
aged 82

My mother with her
sister Stella

Grandfather George Bryant 1924

High House Farm, Huntingfield – haven for hungry
schoolboys 1944

Auster VI

My father, Maurice Rosen, died 1971, aged 76

Early memory – St Paul's Cathedral 31 December 1940
– my father's office obliterated too

Hilary's parents
Comins (Dick) died 1984, aged 87:
Marjorie died 2003 aged 104
Comins was Britain's first Grand Master
and was made MBE for services to chess

Their children – Roderick, Geoffrey & Hilary

Andrew – aged 12   Howard – aged 11   Pip – aged 4

(Painted by William Narraway R.A)

Andrew – second career
– paramedic fireman

Hilary, Howard, Ella, Sue, Lucy, Lydia and me
- at Andrew's fire station Fort Collins 2005

Kara and Shelby, who live in Steamboat Springs

Melanie and Dustin

Pip and Andrew

Andrew in Saudi Arabia

Melanie – showing the Americans how she rode in England

Howard & Sue
- newly engaged

Sue and Hilary, her
new mother-in-law

Howard (groom),
Shelby (usher) and
Andrew (usher)

Sue's & Howard's children

Lucy

Lydia

Ella

Flossie

Howard's Water-skiing Father Christmas – Antigua 1985

Pip, aged 15 – on holiday in Wyoming

Pip

Pete – Pip's partner

Antony   - Pete's children -   Laura

Ollie

Melanie and Pip testing the ice
on our fishpond

Combined operations

Fred

Little Cat

Silou

The Anthil – March 1955 – our first cottage

Old Framlinghamian Summer Ball, Park Lane Hotel,
2 October 1953, Miss Hilary Mansfield, fifth from left

12 metre yacht *Zelita* racing at Burnham

Zelita racing, George Payne "driving", me next to him

Hilary & Anthony - in our gravel garden (2006)

Andrew, Howard and Pip Rosen
invite you to join them in celebrating their parents'
100 years of marriage

Noon
Saturday 14th August 2004 at

**Blackberry House, Cleves Lane
Upton Grey, Hampshire**

RSVP: Six Chattis Hill, Spitfire Lane, Stockbridge, Hampshire SO20 6JS
(01264 - 810135)

Swimming   Tea: 4.00pm

SERVING THEIR MAJESTIES - THE ARMY

After these two years of totally non-academic accomplishment and thoroughly selfish enjoyment, supposedly attending engineering classes at the Brighton Tech, it was the moment to face reality, end my unjustified national service deferment, and sign up for military service. At that time, 1950, one could choose which of the three services one wished to join: although one's choice was not sacrosanct it was generally accommodated.

I wanted to fly so I took the obvious route and went to the Royal Air Force recruiting office for advice. To my dismay I discovered that at that time it was not possible to carry out the flying aptitude tests before committing oneself to the RAF. Since I could imagine little worse than being a penguin (that is a non-flyer in the RAF) for the two years should I subsequently fail the flying tests, the army thus became my choice. Ironically a few months later the RAF offered National Servicemen the opportunity to take their flying aptitude tests before choosing their service – thus is one's future decided.

It was to my surprise, and not a little to my horror, that within two weeks of voluntarily ending my student's deferment I received orders to report to Richmond Station in the far north of England. So on 11th October 1950, after a ten hour train journey from Hove to Yorkshire, I, along with about one hundred other conscripts, was collected at Richmond Station by military transport and taken, in an uncomfortable three-ton truck fitted with wooden trestle seats, to nearby Catterick Camp.

This was to be the start of nine months of humiliation, discomfort and near sadism, but which, in hindsight, was a most enjoyable period in my life. Nine years at public school had provided a good grounding for the strict discipline encountered: I was young and very fit, and the competitive nature of the training built up an amazing *esprit de corps*.

There were one hundred and twenty new recruits in our batch and we were divided into four squads of thirty and allocated our accommodation. These were black Nissan huts which had been condemned for human habitation after the First World War ended, thirty two years earlier. In each bare wood floor-boarded hut there were two black stoves which had to be black-leaded before every morning's inspection, the floor had to be polished daily too. Each squad had a sergeant and lance-corporal in charge and these were effectively our masters for the next four months of basic training.

Having dumped our minimal civilian bags in our hut, it was off to the quartermaster's stores where we were kitted out with an inevitably ill-fitting army uniform, including the roughest khaki shirts that could possibly be imagined. One could wear one's own underpants but other than that it was military kit throughout. Then down to the dining hall, still in civilian clothes, to be presented with a typical supper of truly appalling vision and taste. Later in training we became so hungry that we actually ate these meals, if not with relish at least with gusto.

It was already bitterly cold that first night as there had been no time to light the stoves, nor time to draw the necessary coal from the quartermaster's store. At least this meant that we did not have to clean them the following morning, our first full day as soldiers.

We conscripts, as recruits, were in the Royal Armoured Corps but our instructors were in the mightily proud 17th/21st Lancers – the Death or Glory Regiment whose cap badge was a Skull and Crossbones. They were a tank regiment equipped with the Valentine tank which had been designed, in great hurry, in 1939. Many were shipped to Russia during the war.

We had already memorised our numbers (mine was 22424702) - never to be forgotten. Our first parade was, naturally, a shambles: only about a quarter of our squad had been in school cadet corps and thus knew at least the basic rudiments of soldiering, but for the others it must have been sheer hell.

Our squad was an amazing mix, including four conscripts who had spent their lives in the Gorbals of Glasgow. These four were never to go into town without a bicycle chain hidden under the collars of their battle dress blouses, but their loyalty to their fellow members of their squad was total. There is no doubt that throughout their previous lives thieving had been an accepted way of life but within the squad they were as honest as the days were long. One could have left a ten shilling note (three days' pay) on the top of one's cupboard and it would not be touched: but outside the squad anything movable was fair game. This could be very useful when one lost small items of kit – the men from the Gorbals were always able to supply replacements!

There was a medical examination which consisted solely of a cough, allied to a cupped hand, before lining up for the vaccinations. Six recruits in a row, one needle for all, seven jabs each, alternate arms presented for the ever blunter needle. Perhaps it was as well that we had no idea what poison was being pumped into us. A few passed out there and then but the majority of us staggered back to our huts, there to pass out for the next day and a half. For most sufferers, by Sunday lunchtime the jabs were but a bad memory, but for a few the ill effects lasted much longer.

Monday was when the instruction in the bulls*** really started: the two stoves were black-leaded and polished daily and, truly, so was the coal on the top of the bucket! The wood floor was wax polished daily and "bumped" with long-handled hand polishers: windows were cleaned at least weekly. We had four blankets, two sheets and a pillow all to be folded in a particular way: kit had to be displayed in a meticulous way too: after being blacked with Kiwi shoe polish, spare boot laces had to be coiled like Catherine wheels and held by white cotton: best boots took at least four weeks to be brought up to what was laughingly called "a satisfactory state" - first one applied a whole tin of black Kiwi polish (it had to be Kiwi) to each boot then, after setting fire to this (truly!) the "spooning and bulling" really started: not forgetting the frequently applied very hot iron and lots of spit and polish: one could literally see one's face in your best boots but they were of course completely ruined for their actual use.

All this bull was before breakfast, the best meal of the day. Even army cooks, mainly national servicemen who hated cooking, found it more difficult to ruin this meal compared with what they achieved with both lunch and supper. The local NAAFI canteen was out of bounds to recruits for their first three weeks of training but after this it was a major source of sustenance.

This discipline had a truly remarkable effect upon us all. At the end of the first month the squad really was a team, proud of our mutual dependance and capability and our smart, nay impeccable, turn-out: yes, the bull really did work: come back National Service – all is forgiven. I cannot believe that anyone was not improved by their two years service.

My most famous colleague in my squad at Catterick was Tam Dalyell who, in 1962, long after after National Service in the Royal Scots Greys and schoolmastering, became a Member of Parliament and ultimately became Father of the House of Commons. Although I agree with few of Tam's political views I have unbounded admiration for his total honesty: this shone out then, as indeed it did amongst his fellow MPs until his retirement at the General Election of 2005. Although I did many years later hear malicious rumours of a certain Trooper Dalyall being caught dabbling in the freelance coffee market in Germany!

During our training we each in turn had to take command of the squad for marching drill. When Tam was in control he caught us fooling around and put the entire squad, including himself, on Saturday afternoon extra drill – you cannot get more honest than that!

Sport in the army was important and, being a reasonable rugby player and a county hockey player, in my first two weeks of military service I played three rugby matches and five hockey matches for the regiment. This certainly helped in one's selection for being put forward for the WOSB (War Office Selection Board) tests for possible officer training.

All civilian clothes were mailed home soon after arriving at Catterick, or at least they were meant to be. One of my squad knew a family who lived locally and who invited a few of us to the local Hunt Ball where dinner jackets would be required. A couple of the young 17th/21st subalterns looked askance when they thought they recognised a few of their "squaddies" decked out in evening dress. The only problem was that two of us invited to the ball had to report to the regimental transport office at 5.00am the following morning to travel down to the WOSB at Barton Stacey in Hampshire. After a memorable night at the local Hunt Ball we luckily managed to sleep well on the train.

The specific details of the WOSB test have now, fortunately, faded into history but I do remember having to use oil drums, scaffold planks and our rifles to cross a river. Similar initiative tests were later shown in *Dad's Army*, the TV classic, but with less success than I remember we achieved. The two of us from the 17th/21st passed and were selected for future officer training. Now as "Potential Officers" we had to wear white bands around our uniform shoulder tabs, attracting much ribald, but usually good natured, ribbing - usually unprintable - from our squad colleagues.

There is no doubt that we were fit and although I would certainly not volunteer to repeat the basic training at Catterick, at the time it was a challenge, satisfactorily completed. The skill and patience of Captain Ives and Sergeant Sergeant (yes), responsible for the training of the National Service "potential officers", will remain with me forever. These two highly decorated war veterans were a wonderful example to all who were fortunate enough to come under their command.

And so it was that in March 1951, with few regrets, I travelled down to the comparatively sybaritic south and Mons Barracks at Aldershot for four months of officer training. During our basic training with the $17^{th}/21^{st}$ we had been shown films of all the modern anti-tank weapons, all of which appeared to me to be remarkably effective against the Valentine tank, indeed against all tanks. Thus when we had to select the arm of the army in which we were to be trained as officers I elected to be behind the guns rather than in front, thus into the Royal Artillery, the Gunners. Inevitably both hockey and rugby figured prominently in my Mons itinerary.

One day in the gym I succeeded in dislocating my left shoulder for the second time. After my first dislocation, playing rugby for the Brighton Tech against Brighton & Hove in 1948, I had sat in a wheelchair in real agony in the Sussex County Hospital for four hours until the medico had completed his game of squash. This time the sergeant PTI (Physical Training Instructor) asked me if I had dislocated my shoulder before: on hearing that I had, he asked me if I would like him to put it back: Yes, please, I begged: within seconds it was back in place, and no pain at all – later the sergeant received a reprimand from the Mons medico for doing this prior to an x-ray being taken. I was eternally grateful for not only had he spared me hours of pain it but his action had also meant that within two weeks in a sling I was fit again.

It transpired while I was at Mons that there was also a faint hope of realising my dream of learning to fly. Within the Royal Artillery there were gunner pilots flying as Air Observation Officers and it had just been confirmed that this training would be open to a few National Service officers. I was one of the first to volunteer and to be accepted, at least for the subsequent aptitude tests.

Mons proved to be four months of intense training with 2,000 cadets on the drill square at any one time. Regimental Sergeant Major Brittain, the army's most famous Sergeant Major, was in command of all the cadets' drill. Such was his notoriety that he later enjoyed a career in advertising and voice-over work after retiring from his army service.

During my time at Mons the current top film was *They Were Not Divided* in which RSM Brittain played himself. This drew forth his classic drill square remark, "Don't look at me you 'orrible idle little man: if you want to look at me, go to the cinema and pay for it". Another of his bon mots to cadets was "I call you Sir. You call me Sir. The difference is that you mean it!"

There was much regimental rivalry amongst the permanent staff. RSM Brittain was a Coldstream guardsman while our Company Sergeant Major was a Grenadier. On one memorable parade the RSM ordered our CSM Scholey to "Double your squad off the parade ground and you can double off too, you idle lot". Great fun as long as one was fit and had put one's imagination into hibernation.

On one memorable "Best Boot Parade" I was carrying my precious pair of immaculate Government Issue (completely ruined) black boots, which could easily have been used as a mirror, but my CSM was not impressed, he kept tapping them with his brass-bound pacing stick, exclaiming loudly in measured tones, "You haven't got a good pair of boots, I wouldn't do gardening in 'em until I had cleaned 'em".

Whilst at Mons the Korean War, which had started in 1950, was raging and many National Service Officer-Cadets volunteered to serve there. I did too but was rejected because by then I had been accepted for consideration for Air OP flying training which meant that there would only be eight months, instead of the required year to serve in Korea, between leaving Mons and flying training. I suggested that I would sign on for an extra six months service to provide the necessary time scale, but this was dismissed as being "not in the rule book". To this day I am not sure whether I should be thankful or not? Those colleagues who survived Korea are certainly not unanimous on the effect it had on them.

But in August 1951, with one shoulder pip and a new personal number (416666 – not too difficult to remember?) I was posted to the 17th Training Regiment Royal Artillery, a gunner basic training regiment housed in the once luxurious historic Wingate Camp at Oswestry, which was happily situated only three miles from a world renowned orthopaedic hospital, well staffed with attractive nurses and physiotherapists.

My first Battery Commander was Major Freddie Edmeades, wartime winner of the Military Cross, who was famed for going into battle dressed in Hunting Pink and blowing his hunting horn! My initial employment there was to be sent out with a squad of ten recruits and a three ton truck: I spent the first ten days of my Oswestry posting making hay on the Shrewsbury by-pass for the Royal Artillery Saddle Club – perhaps this is where my "agricultural bias" originated?

I thought at the time, and still do, that it was poor military policy for a newly commissioned National Service officer – less than ten months after I had been a civilian – to be posted initially to a training regiment where one had to rely almost completely on one's non-commissioned officers for even the most basic advice on regimental life. All the older regimental personnel, both officers and other ranks, had served during the war, but sadly, without exception, they were reluctant to talk about their experiences, although happy to guide one on how to behave in this novel role.

When I was a prefect in 1943 in the Junior House at Framlingham I had been confronted by a pair of identical twin new-boys. I quickly had to learn that Michael was the one who behaved while his twin Gerald was an incorrigible tearaway. Three years later, as a prefect in the senior school, once more the twins dogged my footsteps.

Now here I was in a gunner training regiment and again faced with the same twins in my first squad of conscripts! I did not tell my NCOs that I had known the twins for nearly ten years and thus was easily able to tell them apart. Both my sergeant and lance-bombardier were full of admiration for my perception - until I eventually admitted the truth.

On 6th February 1952 King George VI died, aged 56: our King's Commission thus automatically became a Queen's Commission and soldiers officially mourned for a month. There was considerable discussion as to the correct procedure until a senior sergeant major, who had been in the army in 1936 when George V had died, gave us the benefit of his past experience. Basically it meant that officers wore black ties in uniform and civvies, while all ranks wore black armbands on their left arms.

Army sport, at that time, was a major part of soldiering and there was great uncompromising competition between the four gunner training regiments to retain any National Service recruits with sporting prowess. Great consternation was caused when our regiment retained, after his eight weeks basic training, a professional footballer, one Geoffrey Twentyman of Bolton and England, who had been, immediately prior to his national service, transferred for the then record transfer fee of £15,000. Indeed the Brigadier, hearing of the dispute, informed his coterie of four colonels that in future he would personally post anyone worth £15,000 or more.

There were so many professional footballers called up for National Service that regimental teams were allowed to play only five professionals at any one time. In our regiment a player would have had to be a First Division player to play in the regimental competition matches. A neighbouring training regiment built an Olympic running track in their camp because the already great runner National Serviceman 2nd Lieutenant (later the Honorable Sir) Christopher Chattaway had been posted there. During my time at Oswestry I played both rugby and hockey for the regiment and also hockey regularly for The Gunners.

A memorable evening was spent at the Woolwich RA Mess when Lord Louis Mountbatten was the principal guest. Ostensibly the dinner was for senior officers only, that is full colonels and higher. However it was the 17th Training Regiment Officers' Mess Sergeant, who was renowned for his skills at organising prestigious functions, who had been called to Woolwich to supervise this dinner. As a result, in real army fashion, eight subalterns from the 17th went too.

My brother Brian, the 17th Regiment Transport Officer, was at that time coming to the end of his two years' National Service and was the senior subaltern invited and, after the dinner it was made known that Lord Louis would meet the ten most senior officers present. Brian, having imbibed a satisfactory amount of port, decided that he would add to this list and introduce us subalterns as well: this he did, much to the amazement of the Generals present! A coincidence was that Lord Louis's ADC that evening became a close friend some twenty years later and he revealed that Lord Louis had been rather surprised at being introduced to the eight very junior officers: "probably some strange army tradition", he had decided.

In 1951 there was a shortage of Army pilots in the Territorial Army Air Observation Post Squadrons since many in these squadrons, who had flown during the war, were becoming past their sell-by dates. It was thus decreed by those on high that National Service Gunner officers could volunteer to spend the last nine months of their regular service in training as Air Observation Post pilots at RAF Middle Wallop, with the obligation of serving in one of the five Territorial Army Squadrons on demobilisation.

As my Wallop time approached it was required that potential army pilots must pass the official RAF Aptitude Tests at RAF Station, Hornchurch – the first time that Army flyers had to be tested in that way. As it happened, thanks to too much sport and a recurrent dislocating shoulder, when I attended the tests at RAF Hornchuch Test Centre I had my left arm immobilised, plastered to my body, but I passed all the required aptitude and medical tests until my final medical examination, which was for 'hearing'. The RAF squadron-leader doctor seeing my immobile left arm decided I certainly could not fly and announced, "Failed hearing: come back in six weeks." I did, and I passed and was therefore called to attend flying training at Middle Wallop, Course 86.

My first military flight was in a vintage Tiger Moth on 10th March 1952. Since my arm (and my hearing!) were now in good order the next nine months were some of the most enjoyable of my life, being paid by Her Majesty to be trained as an aviator in control, well sort-off, of the high-winged, single engine, 100mph (downhill with a following wind) Auster.

During basic flying training I had to master the intricacies of the magnificently pilot-friendly Tiger Moths and flew them, relatively successfully, for 56 hours 36 minutes.

Sadly all the military Tiger Moths were soon to be sold for £250 each. Similarly the two squadrons of Spitfires, with whom we shared the Middle Wallop airfield, were soon to follow the Tigers to the saleroom where they fetched less than £5,000 each. Today they would certainly be worth more than a million pounds each. But then hindsight is a wonderful thing. Should I have sold my 1923 25hp Rolls Royce on leaving Mons OTU in 1951 for £250?

All pilots under training had their moments of terror, some we were prepared to admit to, others we kept locked in the deep recesses of our minds until we had safely acquired our wings. It was always said "There are bold pilots. There are old pilots. But there are no old bold pilots".

My own particular moment of truth was on a solo stalling and spinning exercise: having completed the necessary exercises in good order, I looked at my watch and saw that I had another forty minutes of flying time to fill in before lunch.

I decided that I would practice recovering from a spin without using engine power, a novel venture not yet taught me. Having climbed up to 2,000 feet above the obligatory height for these exercises I duly stalled and spun. I put the rudder opposite to the direction of spinning and the stick hard forward to recover flying speed, but instead of recovering I found myself hurtling earthwards upside down, altimeter seriously unwinding. Now this was new and I had certainly not been in this situation before. So the obvious, at least to me, remedy had to be to pull back hard on the stick and hopefully pull out of my long sweeping upside down dive.

This I achieved, but only when a meagre 800 feet above the once again friendly Hampshire countryside. I was so shattered that I flew back to Wallop, landed in the furthest corner of the largest grass airfield in Europe, and sat there shaking until it was time to sign in from my "successful" sortie. Later I would be taught that I should have "rolled out" of the dive, but at least I was alive to tell the tale.

The basic wing flying instructors at Wallop were all Royal Auxiliary Air Force ex-wartime flyers who had been called back from civilian life during the Korean War, thus releasing the regular RAF pilots for front-line duty Each of these instructors had many thousands of instructional wartime hours. One had clocked up the amazing total of more than 10,000 hours instruction on Tiger Moths alone. "Instructors' half-hour", at eight o'clock every morning, during which instructors had the Wallop airspace to themselves, was memorable, not only for the lack of accidents, for there was nothing they could not do with these machines.

Having successfully completed Basic Flight it was on to the classic Air OP aircraft, in this case the Lycoming engined Auster Mark V, a dual control two-seater high-winged monoplane capable of very short take-offs and landings. Although not as "user-friendly" as the venerable Tiger Moth it was a most enjoyable flying machine and it was with some regret that, after 55 flying hours in the Vs, I had to change aircraft again. This time it was to the Auster Marks V1 and V11, the former a solo machine where the observer sat in a seat in the back facing towards the tail. The V11 was a dual control aircraft similar to the V1, but heavier and thus requiring more space for take off.

In spite of managing to shorten three propellers, all in Auster Vs, during my training, becoming known in the process as "Prop", I passed out from Wallop with 170 hours flying, of which one third were under dual instruction. I also married the sister of a fellow Wallop officer – but that's another story……

My first "anti-prop" exploit, my first solo Auster flight in strong winds, was because I hadn't realised that in very high winds it wasn't necessary to land with the brakes full on to complete a "short landing". But if one did I proved that it was possible to stop in fifteen yards, albeit with a rather sad propeller and stressed engine. The wooden centre of this bent propeller now hangs on my office wall, centered with a clock.

My second exploit, two weeks later, was when taking off from a relatively short field, thus brakes-on against maximum power, a partridge rose up from the ground and was hit by the tips of the propeller, removing six inches of wood from each end, necessitating an aborted take-off. So it was now two props ruined, only one acknowledged to be my fault.

Then, the very next night, after my first solo night flying landing, as I was taxying for a second take-off, I failed to appreciate that there was another Auster stationary on my route: the result was two written-off Austers. I still maintain that the other Auster, piloted by a very senior Major, must have had a defective rear light.

In spite of these mishaps I duly passed out, having won the coveted Station Commander's Flying Trophy, on 2nd October 1953, wearing my Air OP Wings with pride from then on.

Since the flying bug had caught me, I persuaded the powers-that-be to allow me to extend my National Service by another six months, thus being able to fly about another 100 hours with 652 Air Observation Post Squadron, based in Detmold, Germany. This was the first time a National Serviceman had been allowed to extend his service by six months.

So I spent a most interesting time flying in Germany, in Auster Mark VIs and VIIs, especially because at that time, in the early fifties, the Soviets were building the massive death strips between East and West Germany.

In addition I found time to play hockey and rugby for the Squadron and, as a result of further shoulder dislocation, spent a few uncomfortable weeks in Rinteln RAF Hospital after a very successful Putti-Platt operation on my left shoulder. The Rinteln hospital had been used during the war by the Nazis for their genetic experiments.

The only pain I felt following the operation was from the four-hourly injections of penicillin which, in those days, was thick goo which was administered through a large diameter hollow needle: the nurses quickly ran out of new places in which to inject it. After my operation, with my left arm immobilised and strapped tightly to my body, it was still compulsory to have some form of "occupational therapy". Much to the surprise of the occupational therapist, I choose "embroidery" and was presented, sceptically, with a pristine tablecloth and a tray cloth, complete with the necessary silks and needles. Soon news flashed around the hospital of the one-armed officer in Ward Ten who was an embroidery expert. In reality the squadron adjutant's wife, a brilliant needle woman, visited me every day, returning one piece of embroidery and taking the other. I basked in the glory and never did own up to the truth.

As the only National Service pilot in 652 Squadron I was treated as the one needing the most care and attention from the families of my fellow, all regular service, officers. Indeed during Christmas 1952 I was entertained to seven Christmas Dinners – seven in three days! This is especially puzzling as I also volunteered to be Squadron Orderly Officer on Christmas Day.

As it happened my only duty as Orderly Officer was to deal with the Squadron's Mail Delivery Driver (yes, there was mail delivered on Christmas Day). As he delivered the mail to the Squadron's married quarters it was natural for him to be offered a Christmas drink, unfortunately at every house. A rather inebriated driver was brought before me at ten o'clock in the morning and stretching the obligations of judgment, I sentenced him to "Confined to barracks – for the day".

The Officers' Mess in Detmold, Lower Saxony, shared with the 10th Field Regiment, Royal Artillery, had been built by the Nazis as a Luftwaffe Mess and was unbelievably luxurious: I had certainly never seen triple-glazing before. Added to this the liquor in the mess was "duty-free", thus a gin was one (old) penny, whisky tuppence and brandy three pence: one wrote out one's drinks chit and handed it to the barman.

The new barman was an aged German, genuinely named Fritz: at the first stocktaking after his being appointed there was, even after a re-count, a surplus of seven bottles of gin, four of whisky and one of brandy. On being taxed about this significant error the barmen explained "these young officers write their chits for doubles, but this is not good for them, so I give them singles, much better."

There was a great deal of flying supporting tanks, guns and infantry. At that time we were still the occupying power and could do no wrong. We landed where we wanted. The British tanks too treated the whole country as a battlefield training ground, noting any damage to farmers' crops, for which the farmers would later be generously compensated. Fraternising was not on and so, sadly, no one learned German. We had special discounts if we went anywhere by train but generally met with no animosity.

On one occasion I was deployed to support the 17th/21st Lancers, my old Catterick basic training unit of only eighteen months earlier, now based in Kiel and driving Whippet Scout Cars. Whilst being generally welcomed, especially by those with whom I had played both rugby and hockey for the regiment whilst training with them, some of the junior subalterns were rather offended by one of their recent "squaddies" being their Regimental Pilot, and "only a second lieutenant at that" for all regular pilots had to be at least captains - but it was fun working with them.

Whilst deployed to shoot the 1st Corps guns at Hohne Ranges on Lüneburg Heath I felt that I had to go and see the nearby Bergen-Belsen former concentration camp. It was already a memorial to the many victims, mainly Jewish women and children, who had been held there prior to slaughter by the Nazis.

One of Hitler's most famous concentration camp victims was Anne Frank who died in Bergen-Belsen after being transferred there from Auschwitz in October 1944. As starvation, cold and disease swept through the camp's population, Margot, Anne's sister, developed typhus and died. A few days later, Anne herself, in April 1945, succumbed to the disease, just weeks before the camp was liberated - she was 15 years old.

The European Jews were the main victims of the Nazis and in 1933 nine million Jews lived in the 21 countries of Europe that were to be occupied by the Nazis during the war. By 1945 two out of every three European Jews had been murdered. But Jews were not the only group singled out for persecution by Hitler's Nazi regime. Half a million Gypsies, 250,000 mentally or physically disabled persons, and more than three million Soviet prisoners-of-war also fell victim to Nazi genocide. Jehovah's Witnesses, homosexuals, Social Democrats, Communists, partisans, trade unionists, and Polish intelligentsia were also victims of the hate and aggression carried out by the Nazis. At the Bergen-Belsen camp one could only stand and weep at this memorial to man's inhumanity to fellow man.

One of the lighter and more enjoyable aspects of flying in Germany was the occasional treat of taking part in aerial evasive action, avoiding being "shot-down" by the Meteor jets flying from the RAF Station at nearby Gutersloh. If it was a straightforward one Meteor to one Auster then one stood a better than evens chance of being able to avoid the camera guns from the significantly faster jet by flying slower and lower than they dared. However it was more of a problem when two "bandits" worked together to "destroy" your Auster – with camera guns, thank goodness.

A former Squadron Commander of 652 Squadron had grounded himself for having lost his way while night flying and landing on an autobahn behind a bus. All was well until the bus stopped quicker than he did. Nobody was hurt but there was a great loss of pride. He was posted to command the nearby 52nd Light Anti-Aircraft Regiment. His gunners practised when we used to fly over his Bofors guns, which fired wooden shells which, having recoiled the gun would break up on leaving the barrel - or at least they were meant to. This practice ended when one Auster returned with a hole through its wing – the shell apparently did not always break up.

All too soon the six months of my extended National Service was completed and although I was urged to sign on and seek a Regular or Short Service Commission in the Gunners, Civvy Street beckoned, albeit with absolutely no idea as to what I intended to do with my life. I confess that I was tempted to stay on since my flying experience would have assured my acceptance as a Regular Officer. Subsequently three National Service pilots did sign-on - one became a General, another a Brigadier.

After being demobilised in May 1953 the Territorial Army followed, and I served in both 661 and 662 Air OP Squadrons, based in Kenley and Colerne, subsequently clocking up a grand total of 630 hours flying. Annual camp, lasting two weeks, was usually spent terrifying German citizens, not to mention ourselves.

Twenty-four Austers from one Territorial squadron, flying out to Germany, would occasionally meet up with another squadron's returning planes, all trying to land together at Manston to clear British customs. Since air to ground radios had yet to imposed upon Territorial Army flyers it provided some memorable scenes, compelling one American Top-Sergeant on the ground, viewing the milling aircraft, to announce - "Dis beats D-day!"

Not only did Her Gracious Majesty pay me to fly, adding £1 per day flying pay to our basic salary, but also my flying instructors, especially the remarkable ex-glider pilot, the late Tom Pearce, who had been one of the only three pilots to avoid death or capture at Arnhem, would frequently fly down to my farm to pick me up for a week-end's flying. I could earn more from a week-end's flying than from a week's farm management.

The re-formation of the Army Air Corps in 1957 (which had been disbanded in 1945 at the cessation of hostilities) meant that the Territorial Squadrons now became entirely Army units, the excellent Royal Auxiliary Air Force aircraft and engine fitters mainly retiring, their places taken by Royal Electrical and Mechanical Engineer army personnel.

Sadly the re-formation of the AAC also meant the ending of the all-too-brief intention to convert us fixed-wingers to helicopters. In fact we were now designated as Army Emergency Reserve

(Pilots Pool), we lost our ad-lib flying and no longer attended annual camps as squadrons but simply as individual flyers.

The expansion of the AAC was combined with typical Army planning, including the retirement of many regular Army pilots, which meant that these experienced helicopter pilots were able to fill the Territorial Squadrons, while many of them continued to be employed as Retired Officers at Middle Wallop, often as flying instructors.

In 1961 Jerome Mostyn, another ex-National Service AER pilot, (who, forty years later bought an ex-military Auster V and survived occasional mishaps such as a total engine failure just prior to landing at Cherbourg – after an 85 mile sea crossing!) and I duly reported, after the long, but enjoyable, boat and military train journey via Harwich and the Hook, to my former 652 Air OP Squadron at Detmold for our annual two weeks' flying training. We were not particularly surprised to find that they were not expecting us.

Undaunted, we were checked out by the inimitable and much missed Sam Mousley (who subsequently, through no fault of his own, crashed fatally while overflying the North Sea in a single-engined Beaver aircraft) then presented us with a dual-control Auster VII and told to bring it back, preferably unbroken, a fortnight later. As Sam wrote in my report: "Captain Rosen flies with a lot of dash and élan.....but a heavy pair of feet on the rudders when manoeuvring at low level must be corrected."

It then became a challenge for us two reservists to visit as many Army Air Corps bases in Germany as possible in the time we had. Sometimes we were made very welcome, at another warned off by Verey cartridges - after we had successfully flour bombed the inside of their control wagon!

It really wasn't our fault when, intending to land at Hamburg Airport on a Saturday afternoon, for "rest and relaxation", as we approached on our "finals" as "Number Two in the Circuit -

Number One is an Air France Caravel" we realised that this far faster aircraft was three miles behind us, but quickly overtook us. The British Army's flying credibility was further not enhanced by us discovering that we had a defective left brake, thus necessitating 270 degree turns to the right whenever we were instructed by air traffic control to turn left – on the ground I hasten to add.

Neither do I believe that Hamburg Air Traffic Control, the following morning, one very wet and dark Sunday dawn, ever accepted that we were indeed intending to fly back to our unmarked field strip which was only half a mile from the East German border. In those far-off days we were still the "occupying forces" and a British Army uniform, even for those of us in the AER, commanded considerable respect. We made it, just.

Army flying in those days was great fun, virtually a private flying club, with the occasional excitement. One of the most memorable was spending five hours, together with two other Austers and subsequently four RAF search and rescue helicopters, flying over Dartmoor on a dreary February week-end, searching for "an injured Major John Slim" during Black Knight, a Special Air Service escape-and-evasion exercise. My brother, Brian, was a Territorial SAS and we had organised this exercise jointly.

All was well however, as the Daily Telegraph banner headline the next day proclaimed: "Major Slim missing 24 hours on Dartmoor". "But I recovered", Major Slim said, "and decided to press on and reach my objective" – repacking his yellow recognition panel and failing to tell his would-be rescuers. The estimated cost of the abortive search was in excess of £20,000, a lot of money in those far off days. And the yellow airfield perimeter track marker, which I picked up around my Auster's wheel, landing short in nearly pitch darkness at Roborough, Plymouth, airfield, was reported by the Telegraph as: "He (Major

Slim) put out a yellow recognition panel, which was spotted from the air" - well nearly.

I was released from my Army Emergency Reserve commitment in May 1963 but have managed to attend nearly all the Air OP Officers' Association annual dinners. Sadly as *tempus fugit* we are a declining number, but fifty four very fortunate National Service gunner officers became Army pilots - and a few of them are still flying today. Only now they have to pay for flogging the skies.

Some thirty years later, in 1993, I returned from a business trip to the USA where the company I was working with had their own aircraft. I had piloted, with the owner Karl Schakel beside me, their twin-engined Aero Commander on a low level flight through the valleys of the Rocky Mountains just as the sun was setting. It was a truly memorable experience.

Thus in my enthusiasm on my return I rang the Civil Aviation Authority to enquire what I would have to do to regain my PPL (Private Pilot's Licence), which I explained to them I had surrendered on completing my AER flying thirty years earlier with 630 hours to my credit.

Apologetically they said that they were sorry but I would have to complete five hours of dual flying to regain my licence. The thought of flying solo again with the need for only five hours of retraining was so horrifying that I did not pursue it. I am certainly not surprised at the very high accident rate amongst civil light aircraft flyers.

THE BEGINNING OF MY FARMING CAREER

It has always been assumed during the many years of the Cold War that the Soviets knew that a major part of the British military would be off duty during the weekend, but I always wondered if they realised that the whole mighty military machine came to a halt every Wednesday afternoon – sports time?

So it was that on Wednesday 9th July 1952 RAF Middle Wallop, along with virtually every other military establishment in the UK, ceased, as usual, to function for the afternoon sports – the day after my third broken "prop". I had recently sprained my ankle and was thus unable to represent the Station at hockey as was my norm.

Thus fellow AOP training Course 86 members, 2nd Lieutenant Dick Langley, Captain (Dr) Geoff Mansfield TA and I drove over to nearby Thruxton Airfield to support Dick in his effort to gain his Private Pilots Licence (PPL) by carrying out a cross-country flight in a civilian aircraft.

Course 86 was an unusually mixed collection of five regular gunner officers (four captains and a major), two Territorial RA captains, three National Service RA second lieutenants and two NCOs taking the non-gunnery but otherwise comparable Light Liaison course.

The two Territorials were there as part of an experiment (not to be repeated) which taught them to fly as AOP pilots who would then, on successfully completing the course, be posted to a TA squadron, of which there were five. One of these Terriers was Doctor Geoffrey Mansfield who had been a gunner captain at the end of the war serving in Burma. On demobilisation he qualified as a doctor at Glasgow but since he was keen to fly he volunteered for nine months Wallop training. During his flying course he frequently stood in as locum for the station doctor.

Whilst Geoff and I were waiting in the clubhouse for Dick to complete his cross country flight Geoff chatted up a most attractive bar stewardess. Later he confided to me that he would like to invite her to the Wallop Summer Ball which was to be held in two day's time, but unfortunately he had already invited his sister, Hilary.

I confessed that I did not as yet have a partner organised and would, very selflessly, take his sister off his hands - if he paid for dinner! He accepted with alacrity and thus it was that on the Friday evening I was introduced to his attractive young sister, wearing a fetching strapless sea-green ball gown (complete with bustle – the current fashion) and with the then de rigour long white gloves. We men were, of course, the epitome of well turned-out officers in full Mess Blues.

After dinner, Geoff announced that he was going to Thruxton to collect his partner. Hilary was somewhat surprised to hear of this change of plan but by then it was a fait accompli and Hilary had to make the best of it! Actually she confessed (much) later that she had thoroughly enjoyed our evening together.

However – and this is where there is a slight difference between Hilary's version and mine as to what happened next – a few days later I telephoned Hilary, who was living at home in Carshalton Beeches, but working in London at the Royal Copenhagen Porcelain Company in Bond Street, earning the then princely sum of £7.10.00 weekly, and invited her to the theatre. Hilary's story is that she was so amazed at the audacity of this young man that she accepted, although she had already politely written to him thanking him for a lovely evening at Wallop but telling him that there was no future....since she was involved elsewhere. I never received that letter – was it fate?

So borrowing my father's rather smart Standard Vanguard – complete with front bench seat – I took Hilary to *Twelfth Night* followed by dinner at the then fashionable *L'Ecu de France* in

Jermyn Street, managed by the father of one of one of my fellow officers at Oswestry, thus ensuring that we received red carpet treatment. Hilary always maintained that the car, Shakespeare and *L'Ecu de France* was a confidence trick since I had nothing but my Army pay and no plans for the future. Dinner, I recall, came to £4.10.00 including a full jug of Pimms. From then until I completed my Wallop course in October 1952 and then posted to Germany for six months, Hilary and I spent a lot of time together, the dashing Scot with whom she had been involved receiving 'the letter' this time.

Coincidentally Geoff completed the course and passed out with me in October 1952 and was duly posted to his Territorial squadron, 666 based in Glasgow. To his disappointment two years later he was informed by the Ministry of Defence that they had just realised that he was a doctor and therefore if he was recalled to the army it would be as a doctor and not a pilot – therefore he was ordered to stop flying immediately. At least Her Majesty paid for him to learn to fly but why had he been accepted in the first place?

During my six months in Germany, apart from Hilary, (and there were effectively no telephones in those days) numerous letters certainly brought us closer together and when I returned to England in April 1953 we saw a lot of each other.

Hilary amazingly did not seem to be perturbed that here I was, a 22 year old ex-army flyer with absolutely no plans for the future. She even tolerated my, thankfully short-lived, thoughts that I might become an insurance salesman – but perhaps she knew that even the thought of all that money would not entice me in that direction.

Suddenly, with no warning, my "Good Granny" died, much loved and much missed by all. I think that it was when I went to her funeral and mingled with the rather self-satisfied farming

Suffolk folk that it occurred to me that perhaps a career in agriculture could be worthy of investigation.

Thus I approached the School of Agriculture at Plumpton, East Sussex, to see if they would take me on their one year course in Agriculture. As I was an ex-serviceman they really had, by law, to accept me in spite of there being no vacancy and in spite of my not having carried out a year's work on a farm. They offered me a place for September, in just three months time.

Living in my father's house in Hove I kept myself provided in the necessities of life by flying whenever possible with 661 Air Op Squadron, R.Aux.A.F at Kenley, one of the most famous Battle of Britain aerodromes. Training provided the perfect reason for any flying and I even transported my brother Brian, who was in the Territorial SAS, to and from the Isle of Wight, where he lived, to London for a series of examinations – all good, well paid, flying training. In the last eight months of 1953 I flew a total of more than a hundred hours.

In September I started at Plumpton together with another hundred students, of which six of us were ex-service, the remainder seemed horrifying young, mostly straight from school, some as young as sixteen. It was obvious that most of these young ones, nearly all the sons and daughters of farmers, looked upon their year at Plumpton as a welcome relief from the drudgery of helping out at home.

Included amongst us oldies (i.e. over twenty years old) was an ex-National Service RAF fighter pilot. Since he was a member of the reserve he was able to fly with me in my military Auster and we used one of the college fields as our landing strip. This demonstrated to him just how very different it was flying Austers compared with fighters, especially when we carried out beat-ups of Plumpton which would have been a court martial offence in a fighter.

Being a complete farming ignoramus, for somehow walking behind a pair of Suffolk Punches rolling a field aged about twelve did not provide much agricultural education, I found the very basic agricultural instruction most useful. At least I was taught to tell one end of a cow from the other for in those days the schools of agriculture taught far more practical farming than theory.

In addition to the work there was the sport in which Plumpton did rather well in spite of the casualties which mainly occurred when playing mixed hockey - it was the men who suffered. My transport was a 1928 home-painted vivid yellow Armstrong Siddeley which had cost me my whole year's flying bonus, £80 - a vital necessity for getting to Carshalton to see Hilary at week-ends.

On 19th December 1953, my 23rd birthday, having borrowed £2 from Hilary's father, I took her out to the Box Hill Hotel for dinner and, after a bottle of wine, asked her to marry me, to my delight and mild surprise she accepted. It must have been love for I was no catch. Her father said that it was the best £2 investment he had ever made. We decided that we would get married as soon as I completed the course in July, assuming I had found a job.

A large proportion of the rest of my time at Plumpton was taken up applying for every job advertised in the farming press. *Plus ça change, plus c'est la meme chose* - little changes in the farming world in some respects, for I sent off eighty-four job applications, every one with a stamped self-addressed envelope included - only three farmers had the decency to reply. Of these one had not read that I would be married and would thus need a house, another after interviewing me for a dairy herdsman's position offered us a flat over a fish and chip shop in Sidcup – which we politely declined.

Then our saviour, an offer to be head tractor driver, of two, on a 320 acre farm in Gloucestershire, owned and run by Major Peter Phillips MC, who offered me the job before even interviewing me because during the war the Air OP had helped him fighting with his tank regiment in Germany.

By now I had exchanged the Yellow Peril for a more practical, very smart, 1936 Austin Ten, BLO 400, the *Bloggin*. In this Hilary and I set out on the long trek to look at the farm and accommodation in Gloucestershire. En route we saw an MG car, UD 5103, which I had built during my days at Oswestry with the help of the Regimental mechanics: we took this to be a good omen. It was.

Ann and Peter Phillips were a charming couple with two children, Mark and Sarah. Mark, aged six at that time, hated horse riding but his mother insisted and one can only marvel at where it ultimately got him, the husband after some years of HRH Princess Anne.

"Our" cottage, which we named the Anthil, was a lovely timbered cottage in an isolated orchard (very romantic) but with neither electricity nor an indoor loo. It was badly in need of major decorative work too, but it did have mains water. We were told we could use the bathroom in their farmhouse every evening, only five hundred yards away. And this we did.

After all the hopelessness engendered by potential employers not even bothering to reply this job appeared like a miracle and meant that we could now plan the wedding for the 5th August 1954, just four months away.

All the ex-servicemen at Plumpton passed out with credits in July 1954 while the general level of achievement amongst the younger contingent emphasised the absurdity of taking children straight from school into tertiary education.

Our wedding at St Peter's Church, Woodmansterne, Surrey on 5th August 1954 was attended by about 150 guests with a stylish reception following at The Grange, Wallington. My parents-in-law (Comins Mansfield, was a quiet gentle man, subsequently President of the World Chess Problemists and described in a biography as "A genius of the two-mover") did everything to make the wedding a truly memorable day, and indeed it was.

My father-in-law was as a very methodical man and he listed all the wedding expenses and these records are a wonderful reflection of 1954 costs. The total came to £236.10.7. Included for example were the two bridesmaids dresses totalling £10.11.2: Hilary's wedding dress £26.5.0: two trousseau frocks £13.0.0: a magnificent wedding cake £7.15.0: champagne & sherry £25.0.0: reception £58.14.0 and so on. I see that the watch which Hilary gave me, and which I still have, cost £11.14.4.

Then it was away to the Angel Hotel in Midhurst in my father-in-law's Jowett Javelin. The bill the next morning for dinner, bed and breakfast came to £4.2.6, including a bottle of wine costing one guinea, and inexplicably £0.2.6 for garaging the car.

My uncle's 12-metre yacht *Zelita,* on the Hamble was our home for our week long honeymoon. This sounds more glamorous than it was for not only did the yacht remain firmly anchored in mid-stream but we spent a great deal of time catching rainwater through the leaking skylights. Happy days.

From there, with a princely six pounds remaining between us, we returned the borrowed Jowett and drove up to our new home in Gloucestershire in the *Bloggin,* and took up residence in the *Anthill,* our home for the next twelve months.

The basic wage for a forty-eight hour week was £6.1.0, less six shillings rent for the cottage, but I earned 2s 6d (12½ pence) an hour for overtime. Also Hilary's secretarial skills were utilised by Peter Phillips, Secretary of the Ledbury Hunt, and she earned 2s 6d an hour. It was tight financially but we were newly married and faced the future with confidence, Hilary selling her carefully assembled and much loved stamp collection towards extravagances, such as the Sunday joint. We were young, fit and happy, and looking optimistically to a better future.

Once we were through the 1954 harvest and, even with the first Claas combine to be imported in to England in 1946, we seldom managed more than three acres of corn a day, we worked on the *Anthill* to make it habitable, after a long day on the farm.

In January 1955 I joined 662 Air OP Squadron based at Colerne, near Bath and the Commanding Officer used to fly the fifty miles to the farm to collect me for a very well paid weekend's flying. In the following nine months I managed to put in nearly ninety hours, the pay for which considerably helped our budget.

Then out of the blue in July 1955 arrived an invitation from one of Britain's best, and certainly tidiest, farmers, Reggie Harvey of Tannington, Suffolk, (only five miles from Framlingham) with the invitation to manage his 1,200 arable acreage. To say we flew there was a slight exaggeration but we arrived on his doorstep quicker than a letter would have taken. It appeared that he felt that we had struck up a rapport with him when I visited his farm just before we got married, while spending a week-end at my uncle's farm nearby.

It was agreed that I would start with Reggie Harvey at the beginning of October and we would live in a very comfortable, but huge, rectory in the middle of the farm. Reggie and Daisy Harvey had two sons: Robert who managed the pig operation, the largest in Britain fattening 30,000 hogs annually, and Tony, who, aged 18, suffered badly from asthma and had had to leave school at sixteen. My pay was to be £10 a week plus free house and free pork, since Reggie was the largest UK pig producer! We left the Phillips farm with some regret for although it had been a hard year both Ann and Peter had become friends.

I rejoined 661 Squadron at Kenley and fitted in another thirty hours between leaving Gloucester and arriving in Suffolk. This included, on 28 September 1955, one exciting flight in a Chipmunk, a two-seat in tandem trainer capable of full aerobatics which were not allowed in an Auster. The new squadron adjutant was Flight Lieutenant Tony Alder who had recently earned a DFC in Korea. Brother Brian was on an SAS exercise near Watton in Norfolk, so Tony and I decided to join in and flew in to RAF Watton airbase, full of active V-bombers. There we were met by an SAS open Land Rover, complete with a gun at each corner: the guards on the RAF base were rather in awe as these SAS troopers swept into the top-secret airbase.

After lunching with the SAS in their tented mess, complete with the damask tablecloths and regimental silver, the armed jeep returned us to RAF Watton. Then flying the Chipmunk back to the SAS camp Tony decided to carry out a spectacular beat-up of the troops. I just sat in the front seat not daring to touch a thing as Tony gave a brilliant flying display which is still remembered to this day by my brother and others present. I learned that it is possible to fly an aircraft with a thirty-four feet wingspan between two trees which are only twenty feet apart – quite a challenge.

We moved into the rectory (named Seven Oaks) on Harvey's Braiseworth Hall Farm and spent a week settling in before I started work on Monday 3 October 1955. The first week went well since I found it easy to gain a rapport with the genuine Suffolk farm workers.

At the end of the week, after work on the Saturday evening, I called in to see Reggie to discuss the next week's programme. There I found a distraught Reggie, almost in tears. "I've got to let you go," he said "Daisy is making my life a living hell. She resents your being here as arable manager as she thinks Tony should have the job". Needless to say I was completely shocked at this totally unexpected bombshell. I asked when he wanted me to leave expecting to be given at least some notice. But no, "You'll have to go now. She is driving me mad." At least he conceded that we could stay in the house until I found a new job.

As I left the office Daisy loomed out of the shadows and grabbed me by my arm and hissed "I don't know how you can sleep at nights, stealing a job from a poor afflicted child". I replied by suggesting that perhaps such a child should not be further stressed by having to run a highly profitable and intensive arable farm.

The next problem was how to break the news to my very pregnant wife. There was no easy way. Our dreams had been dashed almost before they started.

MUDDY BOOT FARMING ON THE SUSSEX WEALD

The next day I discussed my position with some local Suffolk landowners whom I knew but there was little they could do but advise me to let the lawyers handle the matter. Many months later I was paid the handsome sum of £250 in compensation. Ironically some twenty years later when I was rather prominent in farming circles I heard that Reggie Harvey was claiming me as one of his protégées.

But the current problem was where to live and where Hilary should register for the forthcoming birth, due in four months. After much discussion, and after spending a couple of months working on my uncle's Debenham farm, fate played a hand. A friend of my father's knew a stockbroker in Sussex who was looking for a farm manager.

Once more we rushed to meet a potential employer and again apparently struck the right chord. I was taken on by Ronald Wheeler, a bright young stockbroker who was credited with initiating the holding company concept together with stripping out the less worthy assets of such companies.

He had his eye on a 200 acre farm at Rudgwick on the Sussex-Surrey border and wanted my opinion on its suitability. The current income of the farm was totally from the sale of rabbits, but since myxomatosis had struck in 1955 the tenant was having difficulty in paying his yearly rent of five shillings an acre The farm had a large empty but imposing house, an attached spacious flat, a farmhouse, in which the bachelor tenant and his ninety-year-old blind father lived, and three cottages.

It had been on the market for a year for £15,000 but, with the sitting tenant in possession, had had no offers. Before bidding for the property we agreed with the tenant that he would relinquish his tenancy for £2,000: it would be difficult to describe his joy at being offered a sum equal to forty years rent! It did not stop him later reminding us that we had to pay his "tenant right valuation", probably actually worthless - but another £300 settled the issue.

Until I took up my farm management position in January 1956 Territorial Army flying continued to provide a vital income. In 1955 and 1956 Kenley airfield, the headquarters of my 661 Squadron, was being used to make the film based on Douglas Bader's life, *Reach for the Sky*. At ten o'clock one morning (my most useful pilot's logbook, RAF Form 414, tells me that it was Friday 13th January 1956) I strolled over to watch the filming. Kenneth Moore, who was playing Bader, was saluting Muriel Pavlov, playing Bader's first wife, and uttering the words "Goodbye dear, I'm just off to the Palace".

I then flew up to Suffolk, aerial photographing my uncle's farm on the way and landing there for lunch, before returning to Kenley (two hours twenty minutes flying time). I then changed aircraft and spent the remainder of the afternoon practising field and forced landings in the low-flying area (one hour ten minutes flying time). Some seven hours later, back at Kenley, I again strolled over to see how they were progressing. Kenneth Moore, was still saluting Muriel Pavlov, and still saying "Goodbye dear, I'm just off to the Palace". The joys of film making.

So the 200 acre Bury St Austen's Farm at Rudgwick was to become our home for the next fifteen and a half years, during which time I learned a great deal about farming – and farmers - good and bad.

It took a year to complete the building modifications to the main house for the owner's occupation and eight months to redecorate completely the farmhouse (after fumigation) for us. My starting salary was £10 per week, but I had a farm car as well as use of the farm's new Land Rover, a £640 purchase.

Hilary and I moved in to one of the cottages early in January 1956 and lived there until the farmhouse was ready for us in

September: Andrew was born in Guy's Hospital, London on 6th February 1956.

It took me a little less than thirty minutes to complete the thirty mile journey to the hospital in the early hours of the morning, leaving Hilary there with the promise that the hospital would ring me as soon as the baby was born. Andrew was born at 7.20am, soon after I arrived home! The hospital advised that we should ensure that we had a faster car for the next baby! I was told that I could visit that afternoon when a baby was held up for me to see through a thick glass window, presumably Andrew. How things have changed.

En route to the hospital to see my enlarged family I called in on 661 Air OP Squadron at Kenley, complete with a bottle of sherry to "wet the baby's head". A small group of us duly drank a toast to mother and baby. I left at noon for the hospital but the head-wetting party ended, so I was told later, around four o'clock the next morning – not on one bottle of sherry.

My role at Rudgwick really was a wonderful one for I had a completely free hand to find more land to purchase, to buy all the necessary equipment, and to hire and fire. Ronald Wheeler said: "You leave the stock broking to me and I'll leave the farming to you".

At that time the top-of-the-range Ford tractor cost £640, a trailed pto-driven Claas Combine harvester £900, a four-furrow Ransome plough £125, a tipping trailer £100 and so on.

It was obvious that Ronald Wheeler was keen that his farm should be expanded and over the next seven years we bought a total of 1,350 contiguous acres which cost, after selling off the houses, a net £45 an acre. Every acre was tile drained at a net cost, after a fifty per cent government grant, of £10 an acre. We built ourselves five miles of concrete road; later erected a 300 cow zero grazed dairy unit to replace our earlier 50-cow tandem parlour; a grain store; a beef unit; and six new cottages, £3500 a

66

pair, all with central heating which was quite an innovation for farm cottages at that time.

In late 1957 the Lord (Lewis) Silkin, who lived near the entrance of our main drive, raised the question of outside investment in farming in the House of Lords saying: "There is a businessman near me who has spent the enormous sum of at least £67,000 on his farm. He could not have done that using taxed income".

Immediately I was telephoned by the Editor of the Sunday Despatch who wanted to contact Wheeler. The front page headline on the following Sunday read: "Why is this Labour peer pillorying me?.......All I have done is spend money on developing my farm and improving the living conditions of my workers".

I discovered later that the Editor, before purchasing a new house near Letchworth, had asked his friend, the Minister responsible for new town developments, Lewis Silkin, if there was any chance of Letchworth becoming a New Town. On being assured that there wasn't, he was more than slightly annoyed when, within a few months of his buying his house, Letchworth became a Garden City with all the attendant development. Thus is headline news inspired.

As we expanded we placed a high priority on employing first class workers who were rewarded well for their efforts in addition to their being able to use the most modern farm equipment. We also took on the tenancy of a further 400 acres of top grade land at Pagham on which we employed one skilled local worker. The farms prospered and by 1964 we were farming more than 1,700 acres.

Howard, our second son, was born in Guildford Hospital in January 1958 (very quickly, but we had, luckily, purchased a faster car, an MG Magnette saloon) and the two boys had a wonderful boyhood, healthy and motivated. By the time Andrew was ten the two of them were insured by the NFU Mutual to drive Hilary's Mini around the farm roads, delivering milk from our dairy to the cottages of our employees, now totalling seven. At twelve, Andrew was relief driving one of our two massive self-propelled Claas combine harvesters while I drove the other, relieving the regular drivers while they had lunch. Howard was responsible for mowing the many acres of drive-side verges using a ride-on mower and they were certainly beautifully manicured.

In 1957 there was a great deal of publicity about the wonderful feeding value of the new variety of maize which had a high carbohydrate value, high dry matter but low protein. Complementary, or so I thought, to this, kale had a high protein and low carbohydrate feed value with high moisture content. So with the new forage equipment available I decided to grow 3 acres of each and make a test clamp of mixed silage.

We cut with a Lundell forage harvester, alternately three loads of each crop and, having borrowed a Lundell blower, were able to fill a clamp with about 200 tons of this mixture. Six weeks later I sent a sample to the National Agricultural Advisory Service (NAAS), later to become the Agricultural Development and Advisory Service (ADAS), laboratory at Reading. A few days later an excited scientist telephoned me to say we had made "the perfect silage" and could he come and collect a check sample. This too came out as "the perfect silage".

In spite of this perfect analysis there was one problem with this perfect silage - not one of our animals would eat it! We tried it on milking cows, dry cows, young heifers, even beef steers. We covered the silage with molasses, then aniseed. But no, nothing would touch it: even mixing minute amounts of this "perfect silage" proved to be a bar to consumption of any food. We had to dump the entire 200 tons.

But in spite of this slight contretemps with the NAAS advisors I had nothing but admiration and gratitude for their friendship and help. Throughout my early farming career I was fortunate in experiencing unlimited help from both the Ministry advisors and also from most of the commercial firms with whom I dealt. Indeed it was the local NAAS machinery advisor, George Tooby, who introduced me to the first forage harvester to come into Britain which was to have such a great influence on farming methods.

In those days of prosperous farming there was a close relationship between progressive farmers and advisors in general. Sadly it was the less progressive farmers who really needed the advice but seldom asked for it, in spite of it being free.

I well recall one farmer sneering at me: "Consultants" he said "consultants? I don't need consultants – I already know how to farm better than I do." He was only half-joking.

Similarly the commercial companies generally employed experienced advisors and salesmen who were usually able to give unfettered advice. One exception to this was the way in which the chemical company Fisons resented their outstanding representative, John Metcalf, recommending the most suitable spray chemical to use, irrespective of which company manufactured it. They could not see that because of this unprejudiced advice John was respected by all and that Fisons gained considerably from this. He later left Fisons and became a director of a local agricultural supply company.

During the very wet harvest of 1958 our barley crops were so badly laid (flattened by storms) that the combine header would not get under the crop to lift it on to the cutters and thence into the threshing drum. Thus extreme measures were necessary and we drove the Lundell forage harvester in front of the combine picking up the whole crop and blowing it down on to the combine table – at least we saved the crop.

I think it was this that convinced me that the agricultural industry had gone wrong, worldwide, in developing the conventional combine harvester. Since more than half the cereal crops grown in Britain were used for animal feed how much more sensible it would have been to have developed the forage harvester to harvest grain: once having collected the whole crop it would then be much easier to work on it in a shed – especially when using the entire crop for feed.

After attending a small local pre-prep school both boys went as day-boys to Cranleigh Junior School, five miles away, where they both thrived. Andrew became a boarder in 1966 and Howard missed his brother so badly that he informed the headmaster, prior to asking his parents, that he would be boarding next term, which he did.

By the early 1960s the farm was running well and even known nationally. We were achieving our objectives in every direction and I therefore had time to become involved in more off-farm activities.

I had intended to work my way up the slippery NFU ladder but quickly became disillusioned at the first step when the members of my local Horsham branch refused to endorse my nomination by John Christian as vice-chairman because "a farm manager can have no idea of what real farmers need". Although I have remained a member throughout my life I never sought NFU office again. I took an active part in the Surrey Grassland Society which, in 1954, had become the first county branch and learned a great deal from some of the most progressive grassland farmers who led national thinking in utilising grass for milk production.

In 1956 we bought the second forage harvester imported into Britain from America and I had become the accepted "guru" on its multiplicity of uses. I was especially keen on using it for haymaking as a means of accelerating the drying process of the crop in the field.

In 1960 I was invited to give a talk at the prestigious Oxford Farming Conference on "The impact of the forage harvester on the farming system". Everything I prophesied at this function came to pass - but it all took three times as long to become accepted as I had suggested. I have never become reconciled to how long it takes for new ideas to be accepted as standard practice in farming. I later served on the OFC committee for three years with interest and enjoyment.

In 1958 a city-farming friend of Wheeler's gave us an in-calf Jersey heifer as a present for our newly established Friesian herd – this was the result of muddled thinking by a typical "train-farmer", as we rudely, but accurately, described many of the local landowners who earned their living in the City. I was fortunate in that Wheeler accepted that whilst he was a financial wizard he knew little of farming and thus left decisions largely to me. But he felt he had to accept the Jersey gift and she was put in with our own stock of bulling heifers – my first really serious farming error. This was to be the start of four years of veterinary hell in our herd.

The Jersey aborted its calf and was diagnosed with *brucella abortus*, or brucellosis as it was more commonly known. This is a vile disease easily transmitted to humans in whom it causes sickness and severe depression. At one time in the early 1960s it was estimated that more than eighty per cent of "large animal" veterinary surgeons were infected with brucellosis, this contributing to the high level of suicides amongst their ranks.

A great deal of research had been done on the disease and even before the war Aberdeen Medical College had stated that it was the "most serious of all the easily eradicateable diseases". Unfortunately the majority of doctors were little interested in the condition since the symptoms of brucella were virtually identical to those of glandular fever and the treatment was the same, simply rest and massive doses of antibiotic.

In agriculture it needed an acceptance of the seriousness of the disease and the setting up of an official eradication scheme, similar to the very successful one initiated by farmers in the 1930s to eradicate tuberculosis.

At the 1960 Annual General Meeting of the British Dairy Farming Association (later to become the Royal Association of British Dairy Farmers) I suggested that we farmers should put our own house in order and accept the seriousness of this awful disease, as our predecessors had with TB.

Literally I was shouted down, even the chairman, the prominent past President of the NFU, Jim Turner (later Lord Netherthorpe), "invited" me to sit down and keep quiet. At the end of the meeting Jim Turner took my arm "Young man" he said "you are quite right, but you must never cry stinking fish about your own product". This was a typical attitude to be found amongst farmers, bury your head in the sand and no one will see you, and all the problems will go away. Later that year at the AGM of the Milk Marketing Board I was asked to leave the hall after suggesting the setting up of a farmer inspired brucellosis eradication scheme.

But still the disease was left to fester and spread: many farmers had no compunction about selling cows which had aborted through the ordinary cattle marts, thus spreading the disease even further.

At the next AGM of the RABDF in 1961 I again raised the subject and, having become better known after my OFC performance, they listened to what I had to say and as a result set up a committee, chaired by the association vet, John Padfield, to report back within twelve months.

At the 1962 AGM the RABDF carried unanimously Padfield's recommendation that the RABDF should set up its own brucellosis eradication scheme. This was so successful that in 1965 the government took over the scheme and it became the official scheme for the whole country. Much to my surprise I was made a Life Member of the RABDF.

By the mid-1970s the British dairy herd was 89 per cent clear of brucellosis and Britain led the world in this important research.

Sadly this was too late for many of the Cheshire dairy farmers who had had to re-stock after the terrible Foot-and-Mouth outbreak in 1967/1968. Immoral farmers happily sold their stock which they suspected to be brucella infected to these hapless purchasers, thus spreading the disease ever further.

Since we had been designing and building our own farm buildings I had long been a member of the Farm Buildings Association and in 1964, as Chairman, had organised the annual conference in Aberdeen, having previously organised Northern Ireland as a venue and also an overseas conference for the FBA in Holland and Switzerland for 84 members – half of whom refused to fly.

Throughout our time at Bury St Austens I played hockey, firstly for the Guildford Hockey Club then, as age took its toll, captaining the Cranleigh Sunday Hockey Club. I was proud to boast that we had we two internationals in the team as well as a famous commentator and sports columnist. Former captain of England cricket, Peter May, could easily have played international hockey if he had had time and John Baxter was already a New Zealand hockey international. Christopher Martin-Jenkins is, thirty plus years later, still famous for his media work. We seldom lost.

On September 10th 1963 we left for our first foreign family holiday, me feeling guilty because there was one ten acre field of barley still to be combined. However two weeks in the secluded village of San Antonio Abad in Ibiza cheered me up. I gather that Ibiza is rather more populous now?

In 1964 I became joint managing director of the newly founded Agricultural Management Limited consultancy company, a subsidiary of the CGA. All my earnings from AML went in to the farm account so as to ensure that there was no conflict of interest with Ronald Wheeler.

Once one has flown as a pilot one never forgets the sheer joy of being airborne in control of a flying machine. So thus it was one year to the day since I had flown my last solo in a military aircraft that I arranged a test flight of a dual-control Sud-Aviation Gardan Horizon. This aircraft was a low wing four-seat monoplane with, supposedly, a good field performance.

On 17th May 1964 I drove to the rapidly expanding Gatwick Airport to meet Paddy, the Irish chief test pilot for Sud-Aviation. From Gatwick we flew the short distance to the farm at Bury St Austen's with the intention of landing in Big Ground, a 23 acre field sown to grass, an approximately square field some 400 yards square. Later that day I wrote this report as a salutary lesson – to me....

Approaching farm landing field (O.S. 171, 172, 173 & 174) said to Paddy: "grass is 15-18 inches long" – Paddy replies: "OK – I will just low fly over field in landing direction to have a look". – direction to be 110° (into wind): flies towards field and LANDS – hard and fast! (No flyover inspection at all) Our two sons, Andrew, aged 8, and Howard, aged 6, climbed into the back two seats, strapped in and bright-eyed with anticipation.

Paddy suggests that I take off: which way?

In an Auster I would take off 300°, to utilise slope, wind negligible – Paddy agrees this is best way.

Full power against brakes: brakes off: slight veer to port, correct – stick in neutral: 250 yards not unstuck, just about to abort take-off when Paddy pulls stick hard back – aircraft lifts/ airborne just - hooter (stall warning) goes – nose up, right wing drops – trees ahead – Paddy hard right rudder – right wing just misses ground – now going 260° - stall hooter continuous – THE LOT – just before right wing about to hit ground, side slips, bounces on undercarriage, I pull on handbrake hard – aircraft stops just short of trees on heading 270° - brakes obviously very efficient.

Paddy, unless 100% confident
should not have landed (later says "Oh I always like to get in first
time").
Should have taken off solo.
Should not have let me drive.

Lundell (forage harvester) cuts take off swath 260° - Paddy takes off
solo – will not land to pick up passengers!

Assessment of 'instructor' – no wonder he bites his nails.
Assessment of 'pupil' – old enough to know better!

To add to the anguish, my once again pregnant wife was watching this from the corner of the field and all she could see was the aircraft taking off, then disappearing downwards out of her sight. Not a good way to convince Hilary that we should have a private plane. Howard complained "we didn't go very high". Little did he know?

Indeed 1964 was a memorable year all round, not least because Hilary was pregnant again with our daughter Pip, who was born on Thursday 18th March 1965, two days before an England rugby match at Twickenham.

Pip has always maintained that we changed her life because we allowed her to be induced so that the doctor could attend the match at Twickenham, making her a Pisces instead of an Aries. And he never did attend the induced birth – too quick.

In 1964 too a group of us founded The Farm Management Association, a national organisation to spread the gospel of economic farm management. We charged £3 for the inaugural conference, including lunch, at the Café Royal in London at which 400 delegates attended. At its peak in the 1970s there were nearly five thousand national members of the FMA.

In 1964 I was offered the chance of a farming partnership in Oxfordshire but, on informing Ronald Wheeler of this unique opportunity, he simply suggested that I went into partnership with him. Still young (I was 33), still naïve, still trusting, we used only one firm of lawyers, Wheeler's, to draw up the partnership agreement. When the agreement differed from what we had agreed, Wheeler dismissed the thought of my taking it to another firm of solicitors who could act for me: "It doesn't matter what the solicitors write, you and I know what we have agreed". In hindsight just how stupid can one get? When we ended the partnership in 1971 this decision not to use my own solicitor was to cost me about £20,000 (about £200,000 today) because by then "we" – Wheeler and I – did not agree on what we had agreed. A salutary lesson in ethics.

There are two aspects to farming. One is the landowning interest and the other is the complementary practical farming side. For example the landowner wants a smart oak post-and-rail fence down his drive, the practical farmer would be happy with a much cheaper, and probably more effective, barbed wire fence.

To overcome this dichotomy of interests we kept a "Black Book", whereby we agreed that all costs which could be attributable unequivocally and only to the landowner would not be assessed in working out the farming profits. As one ultimately learns, a gentleman's agreement is not worth the paper on which it is not written.

In those halcyon days of the late1950s and 1960s it was permitted for farming (including landowning) "losses" to be offset directly against other income, even including so-called "unearned income".   In the first twelve years of Bury St Austen's Farms Ronald Wheeler was able to offset his entire income from the City and paid no tax at all. Farming, or rather landowning and farming, were the perfect way to convert revenue into capital, especially when one remembers that the top rate of income tax was 83 per cent, plus an extra 15 per cent for "unearned income", from shares and similar. Indeed for a short period there was a further 5 per cent surcharge which meant a top tax rate of 103 per cent. No wonder there was an exodus of wealthy people from Britain, at least those who had failed to realise the tax benefits of owning and farming agricultural land.

In 1966 I started a system of co-operative combine harvester use with a Scottish farmer friend. In those days, before the early ripening winter barley was grown in Scotland, the Scottish harvest would never start before the beginning of September while in the south we would expect to have finished our entire cereal harvest by then.

Scottish farmer Stephen Mackie would purchase a new combine which would be delivered to our farm in Sussex: his driver would come down to drive it making use of the southern factory expertise if things should go wrong. We paid Stephen, in those first years, £2 an acre combined, providing board and lodging for his driver, who would work in conjunction with our own combine harvester.

At the end of August the combine would be winched on to a low loader and would be at work in Scotland twenty-four hours later with a well run-in machine to be operated by an experienced driver. For us of course it provided an extra machine at a critical time. I even continued this system using other Scottish farmers as well, until in 1974 we peaked with five Scottish combines working for Fountain Farming. Then the Scots started to grow winter barley which would be ready for harvesting by mid-July, putting paid to our scheme.

Also, thanks to misguided EEC subsidies, following our entry in 1973, massive quantities of oil-seed rape, which was even earlier ripening, were to be grown in the most unsuitable of locations. Prior to out entry to Europe Britain grew 10,000 acres of oil-seed rape, selling for £33 a ton. By 1976 we were growing 260,000 acres, selling for £330 a tonne.

However one smaller-acreage Scottish farmer, who drove his own machine, so enjoyed his visits to the south that he left one combine harvester on our Hedge End Farm near Blandford,

Dorset, and came down every year until 1984 to drive it. He did remark that it gave his wife a welcome break too.

In 1967 I was awarded a Nuffield Scholarship to spend ten weeks in the USA studying "The management of large scale dairy farming". At that time the average UK dairy herd size was 46 cows, a top herdsman earned £20 a week and 78 per cent of herds were still milked in cowsheds. Our herd at Rudgwick comprised 300 cows, milked in a herringbone parlour and the average wage of each of the three herdsmen was £33 a week.

I received a great deal of historic, but incorrect, advice from the US Embassy in London who actually believed that Wisconsin was their most progressive dairy State and literally laughed at the suggestion that California produced milk. Fortunately a friend, then manager of the Reading University farms, Malcolm Stansfield, had just returned from the USA after completing a Churchill Fellowship Study on Dairying. He was able to advise me of the actual location of the large dairy herds and they were certainly not in Wisconsin which had an average herd size of only 25 cows. The California herd size then averaged 650 cows.

Therefore in 1967 I purchased a new left-hand drive tax-free 2200cc Rover costing £1190, including Rover's running it in for 1000 miles in the UK, before shipping it to New York for £45. There it was serviced and on the 1st May 1967 I collected this "cute little car" –American description – and after one night in the noisy hell of New York set off on my 10,000 miles of study.

The first thing I discovered was that in the US universities agriculture was the chosen subject by many people who had no intention of staying in the industry, but simply because it was the easiest course in which to qualify. When I later criticised the fact that only 5 per cent of agricultural graduates from Maryland University stayed on in agriculture after their degree, I was severely taken to task by the Dean who was confident that the real figure was 7 per cent.

Throughout my travels I received nothing but kindness, hospitality and interest. When I had to stay in a motel the cost was between three and four dollars: a pound was then worth 2.70 dollars. The Rover ran like a dream and caused a great deal of interest since the only American car which was shorter than a London bus on the American roads at that time was the very occasional VW Beetle.

I enjoyed all my dairying visits, which included eleven university farms, but I really did not find any progressive dairy farming until I reached the west coast. There the whole attitude to farming changed. Even then Californians did not subscribe to the strange mystique of the "family farm" being the universal panacea for all the ills besetting agriculture. Farming in California was a business and even then, nearly forty years ago, the production of food was as close to industrialisation as it was possible to get. The largest dairy herd I visited was the Alta-Dena herd of nearly 17,000 cows, where milking continued around the clock. The milkers themselves turning up in their smart cars in suits, before changing in to dungarees for their shift. They milked for eight hours, they showered, and they then went home, smart once more.

A most interesting diversion was a meeting with Russell Mawby, Director of the Kellogg Foundation at Battle Creek, Michigan. This Foundation is one of the most progressive NGOs anywhere. Later Newcastle University took up a non-farm training scheme which I brought back to the UK, but sadly after the initial three years of Kellogg Foundation financial support, Newcastle ran out of funds.

On the arable side the crops stretched from mountain to mountain, the entire San Joaquin Valley was covered in magnificent crops. For example there were 62,000 acres of lettuces being grown contiguously in the Salinas area, alongside 10,000 acres of artichokes. These lettuce fields produced three crops a year, the fields being laser-levelled twice yearly, and there was not a poor crop to be seen. Their only limiting factor appeared to be the availability of water for irrigation and all the farmers recognised that this was to be a continuing problem. In 1967 water in the Salinas Valley cost about $4 an acre foot (264,000 Imperial gallons). When I was last there in 2002 some farmers were having to pay nearly $500 an acre foot, but still they grew superb crops.

In Palm Springs in 1967 there were three golf courses, each using 65 million gallons of water annually. On my last visit there were 124 courses there, each prepared to pay $500 an acre foot for their water.

At the end of my American study tour in July 1967 I sold the Rover with 10, 568 miles on the clock, to a British expatriate car dealer in Los Angeles for $33,750, equivalent to £12,500. However the purchaser asked if I would accept a cheque post-dated to August 1967: I had little alternative but to accept as I was due to depart for Cuba the next day.

Later, back in England in August, the dealer rang me and asked if I could please defer presenting the cheque until October. I was not too worried because in the USA it was a criminal, not civil, offence to issue a bouncing cheque. It was my good fortune that in October our prime minister, Harold Wilson, devalued the pound to 2.40 to the dollar: my cheque was therefore cleared for £14,000 – so the "pound in my pocket" was certainly affected – but positively.

After a fascinating week in Cuba with Dr Reg Preston, the Scottish pioneer of intensive barley-fed beef, where he was feeding livestock solely on sugar cane, I returned home determined that large-scale agriculture was the way farming had to go and could certainly provide significant returns on invested capital.

This was confirmed by our "black book" system which had demonstrated all too clearly that the actual return on the tenant's capital, that is the actual farming operations ignoring the landowning costs, was exceptionally good The seed was planted but with eleven years of working closely with Ronald Wheeler my loyalties, and typical inertia, prevented my taking it further…..for the moment.

In 1968 I was invited by the Technion in Haifa, Israel, to spend two weeks looking at their farming and rural development and to advise them on any possible improvements they could make. My host, Professor Emmanuel Yalan, was a world renowned expert on rural development and so it was indeed a challenge to suggest improvements. The morale of the Israeli nation was at its peak following the successful outcome of the 1967 Six Day War and one had to be impressed by the determination of the people to improve their country.

In 1970 I was awarded a Winston Churchill Foundation Scholarship to study large scale dairying, again, but I was so involved in setting up Fountain Farming that I never did take it up.

At Rudgwick we purchased at auction a renowned twelve year old imported Friesian bull, Doreward Annie's Adema for 1,000 guineas. Then, having obtained a MAFF licence, which had a duration of one month, our vet collected 1,200 doses of semen from him for deep freezing. We approached the venerable auctioneers of pedigree livestock, Harry Hobson & Co, and asked them to sell these doses at the end of their normal Friesian sales and, although they had never done this before, they agreed. They regularly sold lots of ten ampoules for £100, which yielded us a very good return on our original investment. Whether or not the exercise had had a terminal effect I know not, but Doreward shortly afterwards expired.

We then purchased a young Friesian bull Montgomery Winled, altogether a less docile animal. One day the herdsman and I led him out of his pen on two chains (yes, chains) for the vet to collect his semen. Winled decided that this was not to his liking and managed to snap the chain held by the herdsman. Thus I was left holding an angry bull on a chain, which is not an enviable position in which to find oneself. He turned on me, crushing me against the steel rails of his pen, then placing his horns across my thighs tossed me upwards, fortunately over the rails, less fortunately dislocating my left shoulder, again. But at least there was now a set of steel rails between us and I managed to wrap my chain around these before retiring, leaving the herdsmen and vet to sort out the enraged animal.

When I tackled the makers of the broken chain they said that these should only be used when "showing the animal"? Three lessons emerged from this contretemps: firstly one should only handle a bull using a bull pole, not a chain: secondly that there is no such animal as a safe bull; finally that even a well operated on shoulder joint cannot withstand such treatment.

My shoulder, following this accident, continued periodically to dislocate so in December 1969 I went into St Mary's Hospital for a second Putti-Platt operation which was a great success. More problematical was the pulmonary embolism which occurred eight days later, fortunately while still in St Mary's, where it was rapidly treated.

In 1970, together with the other founders of the Farm Management Association, I helped set up the International Farm Management Association. Our inaugural IFMA Congress was held in Warwick University in July 1971, attracting 650 delegates from more than twenty countries. The IFMA continues to this day holding their Congresses every three years around the world.

Returning to capital land values, it is interesting to compare the £65,000 that it cost Wheeler for the 1,300 acres of owned land after our improvements with the fact that fifteen years later it all went on the market for £3.2 million.

Having worked with Ronald Wheeler, one of the City's leading stockbrokers, for fifteen years I have to report that my share trading with his advice ended with us being exactly financially neutral – no gain, no loss. There is a lesson here surely?

In 1961, having purchased Waterlands Farm, we decided to clear a wood which was over the site of Stane Street, a Roman Road, originally running from London to Chichester. We found the original road some four feet down in perfect condition. Later wild oats were to grow along the line of the road – an interesting throw back to many centuries earlier.

However at the end of the 1960s Ronald Wheeler unilaterally decided that Carl, his 21 year old younger son, should take over the farm immediately upon leaving agricultural college so ending a very happy period of our lives. Carl's future had been discussed over the years but it was always "Carl will farm elsewhere" so it was a nasty surprise at the time but one that proved most fortuitous in the long-term.

FOUNTAIN FARMING

Thus yet another era ended so we decided that I should set in motion my scheme for a tenant farming company using public company funds, which would show a significant return to its shareholders. My first thoughts were to approach the well-known entrepreneur Jim Slater who was then, having successfully taught the City a great deal in money terms, talking of starting a farming operation.

Fortunately before I could do this, I showed my proposals to a friend (coincidentally a decorated wartime Air OP pilot) who I knew was "something in the City". John Eldridge was then the Managing Director of Matthews Wrightson, reputable insurance brokers, which already had a forestry investment company (headed by another ex-army pilot!).

John had, as company actuary, in 1957, initiated the renting of the newly built tallest building in the City, the ten-storied Fountain House in Fenchurch Street. He had negotiated a rent of double the going rate of ten shillings a square foot, which drew considerable criticism from some of his fellow company directors. It was not until later that they appreciated that he had agreed to a 99 year lease, with no rent reviews: twenty years later the lease was sold for £46 million.

John was as enthusiastic as I and, with a rapidity that impressed everyone, Fountain Farming was established with me as Managing Director at a salary of £5,000 a year. I had declined the offer of a salary of £3,500 plus taking a percentage of the profits as I knew, from previous experience, that there was no way in which the objectives of the company and mine could be reconciled fairly if I was to be paid on a bonus system.

Basically my idea was that the tenant farming company, Fountain Farming, would buy land with vacant possession and, after letting it to ourselves, would then sell the now tenanted land to interested investors. Initially we would target investors who were especially interested in the then 45 per cent death duty rebate for agricultural land and who also sought a reasonable financial return on their investment.

In July 1971 we bought our first farm, the 1,040 acre Chapmansford Farm in Hampshire, paying £312 an acre, the first time agricultural land sold for more than £300 an acre. Historically agricultural land first fetched £60 an acre in 1950, £100 an acre in 1960 and £300 an acre in 1971. It was a top class property which had been owned by the late Sir Allen Lane, of Penguin Books fame, and was equipped with a new granary, dairy unit and two upmarket houses as well as five cottages.

It was also agreed that Hilary and I would purchase the main farmhouse on Chapmansford Farm, in which we were to live, for a price to be agreed by a valuer, of between £20,000 and £25,000. Unfortunately the old boys' network prevailed and, knowing that the value of the farm had already increased by £60,000, a director of Stewart Wrightson bought the farm secretly at the original price we had paid, providing he could have the farmhouse for himself. John Eldridge was especially affected by this provision which meant he could not keep his promise to us and so went all out to make amends. In 1977 Fountain Farming bought the 10,000 square feet "minor stately home" of Moor Hatches in West Amesbury, Wiltshire. Hilary and I purchased the residential two-thirds of it, while Fountain Farming headquarters utilised the other one-third.

Even at the best of times tenanted land is of less value than land with vacant possession, at least since agriculture entered its golden period with the onset of the Second World War. Fountain Farming solved this particular problem by guaranteeing to buy the land back from our landlords at full vacant possession price on Michaelmas Day or, failing that, we could have the option of releasing our tenancy, actually giving the landlords vacant possession.

It must be remembered that until the Agricultural Act of 1995, which allowed any length of term of Farm Business tenancies, all agricultural tenancies were for, at the very least, the lifetime of the tenant. Indeed, under the absurd 1976 Agricultural Act, tenancies were extended for two further generations of tenants: this naturally had the effect of ending the possibility of any new tenancies being offered, until twenty-five years later when the Farm Business Tenancies Act allowed legally binding terms for farm tenancies. Of course, Fountain Farming being a company, our tenancies were for ever – or, in the light of what happened later, with hindsight, I should say for the lifetime of the company.

The objective of Fountain Farming was to make a significant return on our invested capital while at the same time ensuring that the best possible staff that we could find would operate farms of which we could all be proud. One of my proudest memories is that there was never a time when any of the Fountain Farming operations was criticised for its standard of farming.

There was an annual trophy awarded within the company for the Best Kept Farm and another for the Most Improved. These awards were presented at the annual gathering when all staff came together on one of our farms to meet their colleagues with the idea of building up team spirit. Every employee attended, even if it necessitated flying them to the venue and hiring relief workers to stand-in.

There were Fountain Farming ties and lapel badges. The apocryphal story is that on my asking one of the managers why he was not wearing either, he replied "Sorry, I must have left them on my pyjamas". There was a considerable pride in working for Fountain Farming as we were recognised as leaders in man management and practical farming.

Apart from the annual gathering there were local meetings, including sports events. One of the Dorset farms had a considerable advantage on these occasions as they always carried home-made scrumpy as a pre-match libation for their opponents.

We were criticised by those farmers who did not know us for being unfair competition for the "conceptual ideal", the mythical "family farm". We were criticised for our scale, for, within five years we were farming 30,000 acres in Britain. We were criticised by those who envied us. We were criticised, put simply, for being the best. We employed 200 of the very best people in British agriculture.

We employed seventeen managers in Fountain Farming, of whom only three came from a farming background. Our managers were not hidebound by tradition: they stood out for their initiative. They all participated in local affairs, both non-farming and farming. They had to be above average for the competition for all positions within the company was fierce. Whenever we advertised for farm management trainees we would receive scores of applicants – indeed one we rejected (who shall be nameless) went on to become President of the National Farmers' Union!

Every employee, in every position, had to be the best because there were 5,200 dairy cows to be milked, together with the same number of young dairy stock: there were 25,000 sheep, 1,500 beef animals, 6,000 acres of vegetables and 10,000 acres of cereals. Our annual turnover in the first part of the 1970s reached £6 million and the return on our "tenant's capital" was, until 1978, in excess of 24 per cent.

Unlike most farmers, who rapidly write down the value of their tenant's assets, Fountain Farming, as a subsidiary of a public company, had to re-value its assets every year: thus it was on these enhanced figures that we had to show a return. There was no doubt that we were a success.

As the tax laws altered, and it must never be forgotten that the whole structure of British agriculture has continually altered to

87

meet the usually short sighted demands of the British tax system, Fountain Farming altered its means of acquiring land.

After the Second World War nearly 90 per cent of farm land was farmed by tenants and 10 per cent by owner occupiers. It was this system of complementary needs that made British farming the envy of the world in the fifties and sixties.

Then as the fiscal demands on landowners grew, for under successive government they were considered to be the pariahs, many decided to become owner occupiers, until, by 1995, no more than twenty per cent of land was farmed by genuine tenants. Many so called tenants were in reality intimately connected to their landlords, often being tenants in name only of family trusts.

Fountain Farming continued to expand throughout the seventies, both in Britain and, in 1974, in Iran. As UK fiscal demands altered so we modified the ways of obtaining tenancies. For example it soon became clear that many pension funds were seeking better ways of investing their funds so they bought farmland from us, or even in some cases bought the land themselves and let it to Fountain Farming, since they could appreciate the value of proven company tenants. Although we took over existing farming operations we were adamant that we would never employ the "sitting" owner as manager, for obvious reasons.

Our huge scale could sometimes mitigate a problem. In October 1975 in the southern half of Britain it effectively stopped raining for ten months. Conditions were so dry on our southern dairy farms that in May 1976 we transported all our dry stock to our Scottish farms where there was ample grass. The other effect of that drought was an additional cost of animal feed of £350,000 in the following winter to replace the lack of silage.

In 1976 the Electricity Supply Nominees Pension Fund purchased a 25 per cent share in Fountain Farming for £1.1

million, this effectively relieving our parent company, now Stewart Wrightson (metamorphosed from Matthews Wrightson), of any capital investment in us at all. We flew the ESN agents around all the farms on the 23rd and 24th of August in a helicopter. The whole of southern Britain was so parched that even from only 500 feet above the ground it was not possible to tell the difference between cereal stubble and grass. The rains started on the 29th August and fell continuously to such an extent that 1976 turned out to have the "normal" average annual rainfall of 30 inches - misleading.

In 1973 I was invited to join the BBC Agricultural Advisory Committee. From this resulted six years of most interesting insight in to the way in which this great institution, the BBC, works, or not.

During the 1970s being responsible for Britain's largest farming operation I was invited to meet the "great and the good" and others (!) fairly frequently. On one occasion I was dining with the agricultural attachés of a number of countries, including some from the Eastern Bloc.

The Soviet Attaché was sitting on my right while a truly outstanding Romanian, Dr Popov, sat opposite me. The Soviet insisted that I should go to Russia and see the best arable farming. Immediately Dr Popov leaned across and, to my surprise, said "Yes, Anthony you must go to Russia and see their arable farming".

The Russian then said the same about their dairy farming: again Dr Popov insisted ""Yes, Anthony you must go to Russia and see their dairy farming". This vein continued for some time but when the Russian had completed his invitations Dr Popov then interjected "Yes, Anthony and when you have returned from Russia seeing their best you must come to Romania and see how it really should be done". I think it was some time before agricultural diplomatic relations recovered.

In 1976 I joined the Agricultural Forum and remained a member for twenty years. This really was the most enigmatic body since it comprised leaders from throughout the food chain, from the basic raw materials through to the giant supermarkets: thirty members – all men in my time – with colossal personal power and prestige, two-thirds of them were knights or ennobled. But the Agricultural Forum was so frightened of any publicity that apart from being a most interesting and enjoyable talking shop (we dined quarterly at the Hyde Park Hotel) it achieved nothing. It could have been the most powerful representative body that agriculture had ever had, but it was not to be - what a sad waste of potential. Although it continues today it is still as dark and mysterious as it ever was.

In 1978 potential disaster for Fountain Farming struck when our very supportive founder chairman, John Eldridge, a truly gentle man, became the victim of internal City company politics. Whilst on a company flag-waving business trip to Japan the knives back home flashed and he was ousted.

The new Stewart Wrightson chairman presumptive, in total contrast to John, was a self serving demagogue who had no interest whatsoever in any part of the organisation that was not directly under his immediate control. Very quickly all the non-insurance broking sections were discarded and a company which had taken years to put together was decimated. Ship broking, forestry and farming were irrelevant to the new chairman's scheme of personal aggrandisement. Ironically once having wrecked havoc and destroyed a very successful company, he quickly moved on to new pastures, and newer pastures and even newer pastures. I wonder if it is libellous to write that he was the most selfish man I have ever met?

I was commanded to attend upon him at his London office in November 1979. He announced that he was selling Fountain Farming.

"How long have I got to organise the sale?" I asked.

"How long do you want?"

"Two years, until Michelmas Day 1981."

"Why?"

"Because we have forty six tenancies and a farming company is not something that you can easily unscramble".

"I want us to be completely out of farming by the end of September 1980 at the latest. You must write to all our landlords and ask if they will release us from the tenancies by then".

Obviously every landlord would accept this incredibly ingenuous offer because it immediately gave them a premium of the difference between vacant and let land which at that time, as farming economics were generally tight, was considerable.

"If you do this it will cost your shareholders at least a million pounds, the value of the tenancies" I warned him. But his mind was made up, September 1980 it had to be, so I went on to say that I would not do such a damaging and ill thought out deed unless he gave me orders in writing, which he did.

As expected the responses from our landowners was immediate: by return of post the Recorded Delivery letters releasing us from the tenancies flowed in. I had at least insisted in putting in my letters the proviso that they could not "dilapidate" us, which saved us many hundreds of thousands of pounds, since it was all too easy for pernickety land agents to find faults in the condition of the buildings and similar.

I do not think that it helped the personal relationship between the new Chairman and me when a guest at a Stewart Wrightson party asked the chairman if they were a subsidiary of Fountain Farming. I knew our public profile was high, but our chairman was not a happy man.

Together with a banker and my fellow Fountain Farming directors we presented a management buy-out scheme to the chairman. As expected it was refused out of hand. The last thing the chairman wanted was for Fountain Farming to be seen to be a success after he had offloaded it.

I was the tenant of the Prudential Insurance Company of the 1,350 acre Hedge End Farm, near Blandford, Dorset, although we had farmed it as part of Fountain Farming. The chairman insisted that I write to the Pru's agents, Cluttons, asking them if they would allow a new tenant named by Stewart Wrightson to take over the tenancy from me. Nigel Clutton laughed out loud at the naivety of the request, explaining that the tenancy had been granted to me because I was a suitable farming tenant and the chairman's ignorant request was declined. Hedge End comprised 450 acres of goodish land, 450 acres of average land and 450 acres of really appalling land. This latter was pure flint over chalk and should never have been cleared of its trees in the 1940s. We had built-up two herds of dairy cows, totalling 320 and their followers.

The remainder of the Fountain Faming farms were taken in hand by the various landowners and our land agents calculated that these landowners had seen an increase in the value of their holdings in excess of £45 million. Not a bad return in such a short time.

Throughout my farming career I had enjoyed a close and trusting rapport with the media, both national and agricultural: I found that if one spoke in confidence with them then they would honour this trust. Sadly in 1980 this trust was betrayed by a brash young journalist who came to England from writing for the gutter press in Australia. He asked me if it was true that Fountain Farming were selling off all its dairy herds immediately, prior to the sale of the company. I assured him that nothing could be further from the truth and that FF would be sold as a going concern. I told him that it was difficult to maintain the morale of the staffing of our 36 herds in the face of the uncertainty of a sale and that such a false story would damage morale irrevocably, and please not to propagate this untruth.

Sadly this aggressive former "red-top" writer was determined that he had a scoop and printed this lie. Fortunately I had anticipated that he would write his falsehood and had written a personal letter to the 52 herdsmen assuring them that we had no intention of selling the cows separately. It worked and every herdsman stayed with us to the end.

The farming on every farm continued in one form or another with, happily, no Fountain Farming employees losing their jobs. Today, thirty six years later, there is still a group of Former Fountain Farming managers who meet regularly and carry out a great deal of co-operative buying and marketing.

The disorganized sale of Fountain Farming exemplified the short-termism and cynicism of so much of the City of London thinking. They had made the decision to be out of farming by the end of September 1980 and the fact that the shareholders received about £2 million below the true value was irrelevant. Such foolishness did not affect the directors' incomes and who cared about the shareholders? What the shareholders didn't know they couldn't complain about.

As a further example of City greed Stewart Wrightson offered the eight Fountain Farming executives who were entitled to pensions a truly derisory sum which I refused to condone. My complaints were basically ignored, so in 1982 I warned the Chairman that since I held one share in Stewart Wrightson I intended to raise the matter at the company's AGM.

To be fair the chairman accepted my intention and allowed me to protest in front of a full house of about 400 shareholders. I raised the question as to how Stewart Wrightson felt able to advise clients on their pension arrangements when they could not even look after their own ex-employees. After about four minutes the chairman interrupted me to suggest that a better place to discuss this would be in his office to which I did point out that I had been trying to meet him for two years: he assured the meeting that he would meet me.

Two weeks later I met him in his office and his opening gambit was "You don't really think that I am going to give way on this do you?" To this I responded that I would then present myself again at the 1983 AGM. At that minute the company secretary came in and the chairman tackled him with an opening gambit: "Tony, Anthony says that we treated the redundant Galbraith Wrightson (ship-broking) executives considerably better than we are treating those in Fountain Farming – it is not true, is it?"

To my eternal gratitude Tony Sicely replied: "Oh yes, considerably better". I left the meeting with pension offers for my former colleagues three times that which they had initially been offered. And even greater contempt for the Chairman.

Happy days, but once again a new direction in our lives was needed.

Moor Hatches – home and Fountain Farming HQ

Fountain Farming Management Team - 1975

Part of 300 cow Friesian dairy herd at Bury St Austens - 1966

The widest clear-span wooden building in the UK
Boreham Dairy Unit - 1974

One of Fountain's sixteen rotary parlours

Boys' Toys

First Fountain 'greenfield site' milking unit at Wooldings Farm, Hampshire.
Net cost £138 per cow after MAFF grant: including two centrally heated
cottages, rotary parlour, 200 cubicles, silage clamp, 200 yards concrete access
road

Combine harvesters

Occasional views from Chattis Hill Stables

Passing out Course 86 at Middle Wallop 1st October 1952
(My brother-in-law, Geoffrey Mansfield, seated far right)

ROYAL ARTILLERY 1st XI AT FOLKESTONE HOCKEY FESTIVAL – EASTER 1952

1947 – Framlingham beat KS Rochester 11 – 10.

The end of an era:
disbandment parade of 661 Air OP Squadron – February 1957

Food from Our Own Resources

Presented to Parliament by the Secretary of State for Northern Ireland, the Secretary of State for Scotland, the Secretary of State for Wales and the Minister of Agriculture, Fisheries and Food
By Command of Her Majesty
April 1975

LONDON
HER MAJESTY'S STATIONERY OFFICE
22p net

Cmnd. 6020

Food from Our Own Resources – MAFF 1975
(Illustrated by Pip, aged 10)

F.W. 9.7.76

BIG DROP IN FARM OUTPUT

Output from UK farms fell by 14 per cent in the year following publication of the Government's White Paper *Food From Our Own Resources* in April, 1975. This is the largest annual drop in agricultural production since before the Second World War.

The White Paper projected an expansion in farm output of 2·5 per cent a year.

Businesses fleeing from EU taxes

IT IS not only the British who believe that the costs of membership of the EU are hindering company profitability and thus lengthening the dole queues. Many other nationalities are convinced that they would be better off leaving their native lands and setting up elsewhere – especially in England.

The enthusiasm of mainland continentals to move their businesses to England can be gauged by the fact that a club, La France Libre d'Enprendre, has been formed and is based in Ashford, Kent. Offering businesses more freedom than can be enjoyed in France, as the name suggests, has been popular. The organisation already has more than 700 French members; all interested in establishing their businesses in England, either in place of or in addition to their French bases and established businesses. Currently some 255 French members of La France Libre d'Enprendre have set up their companies here; more are moving weekly.

Apart from the frequently quoted comment by members that: "The social environment is much better in England", it is when one studies the comparative costs and taxes of the UK and France that the only surprise is that the headlong dash is not greater.

Currently a married man, earning a salary of £20,000 in the UK, takes home a net sum of £15,132, after taxes and insurance. His cross-channel contemporary would take home £13,550, or £1,582 less than his counterpart in England. In Germany, the equivalent married man's take-home pay would be £14,163.

But it is the unmarried worker who, in both France and Germany, is treated

> "Currently some 255 French members of La France Libre d'Enprendre have set up their companies here; more are moving weekly."

most harshly. With annual earnings of £20,000, a single person would pay £5,060 in national insurance and taxes in England, £6,387 in Germany and a massive £8,350 in France.

It is French companies, however, operating in France, which are even more penalised by their various government-

Businessman, agriculturist and journalist Anthony Rosen describes how continental businessmen are protecting their companies from high EU non-wage employment costs and company taxes by forming companies in Britain.

imposed costs. For example, a company making a profit of £400,000 a year, employing 100 people, each with an average annual salary of £20,000, would in the UK contribute, in taxes and social insurances, £296,500 to government coffers. In France the same company would contribute £977,000, more than three times as much as its competitors in England.

As a convenient alternative to moving the whole business across the channel, French companies are establishing businesses in England which then carry out work for their French masters. The French parent company in turn pays consultancy costs to its English subsidiary which one can normally only dream about.

Thus a legal type of 'money laundering' transfers the profits, on which UK taxes are of course paid, from the French master operations to the English company.

Rather surprisingly, Air France, a French

government owned company, has un-Chauvinistically recently set up its new international reservations headquarters near Wembley, England, where it will employ 300 people. The official reason given for the establishment in England for such a massive investment: "It is easier to find multi-lingual people in England than in France." Less surprisingly, Air France

> ".... it is the the unmarried worker who, in both France and Germany, is treated most harshly."

declines to discuss the reason for the move with journalists.

Similar government-inspired costs pertain in Germany as in France, and only last month RWE, one of Germany's largest electricity companies, announced that it might consider moving its headquarters to Britain. RWE is also reconsidering its investment in a new lignite mining project near Dusseldorf because of increased taxes. Viag, the German tele-communications and energy group, allied itself with RWE's protest to government.

Earlier this year Allianz, the large German insurance group, suggested to the government that the new tax laws in Germany could add DM2.5 bn to its next three years' costs, and that it might well move its operations to either London or Zurich.

But the uncontrolled dash by the French is not confined only to England; anywhere

> "It is estimated that more than 195,000 French citizens have moved to Switzerland to avoid the penal taxation and social costs of their native country."

out of the EU is considered justifiable. It is estimated that more than 195,000 French citizens have moved to Switzerland to avoid the penal taxation and social costs of their native country. One famous French actress explained her move: "The air is purer in Switzerland".

The more optimistic French nationalists believe that if the UK enters the euro monetary system, French and other European nations' taxes and social costs will be reduced to compare with levels pertaining in the UK. Realists appreciate that, like the temporary original English income tax set at four old pence in the pound in 1799 (six years after the French), taxes never decrease. But the realists hope that England will realise the folly of joining E&MU, and remain outside as the final bulwark against the tide of European federalism.

Comparisons of take-home pay in UK, France and Germany				
Annual salary £20,000: 1999/2000 figures				
		NI	Tax	Take home
UK:	Married	£1,656	£3,216	£15,132
	Single	£1,656	£3,408	£14,940
France:	Married	£4,000	£2,450	£13,550
	Single	£4,000	£4,350	£11,650
Germany:	Married	£4,300	£2,087	£14,613
	Single	£4,300	£3,087	£13,613

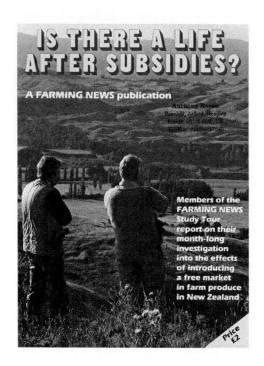

Sponsored Tour of
New Zealand - 1992

Larry Klaas – producer
A Feast Amid Famine
Grand Palace Thailand 1988

Filming Minister John Macgregor for *"A Feast Amid Famine"* - London 1988

Masai Mara, Kenya

Torres del Paine, Chile

Galapagos Hawk

Iguazu Falls

Modern farming?

Cape Town, South Africa October 2005
– The camera never lies?

Rosen as conqueror, somewhere on Salisbury Plain, 1952

PHOTO: ANTHONY ROSEN

Sherkat Sahami Landkesht - 700 miles north-east of Tehran:
40 miles from the Soviet Union: 30 miles from Afghanistan

Iraj Hedayat (far right) – Chairman, Sherkat Sahami Landkesht

The Blue Dome Mosque near Isphahan, Iran

Modern Perspolis

Hilary presents prize to John Haigh
Farmers' Club Dinner - 1978

ENGLAND'S
PLEASANT LAND
Vision & Reality

Anthony Rosen
with paintings by David Mynctt

9,000 copies sold - 1988

IRAN (1973 – 1979)

There was worldwide interest in the rapid growth of Fountain Farming, mainly resulting from the considerable media coverage in both the farming and business presses. One direct result of this publicity was an invitation from the Confederation of British Industry and the Ministry of Agriculture for me to join the UK delegation to the Iran-United Kingdom Investment Conference in Perspolis, Iran, to be held in November 1973. This honour was irresistible, in spite of the daily pressures of running an ever expanding farming empire, and I accepted providing our Development Director, lateral thinker David Rushton, could accompany me.

At the Conference it was clear that the two of us from Fountain Farming were effectively the only agriculturists amongst the sixty UK delegates: this was to cause considerable amusement and even more consternation amongst our hosts, at what turned out to be a largely agriculturally oriented conference.

David Rushton and I flew out to Tehran on Friday 23rd November, the journey, via Paris and Rome with Iran Air, taking a little over twelve hours. One memorable moment was a perfect landing in Paris in dense fog with the English pilot announcing that this was his first entirely hands-off landing. Luckily he told us after he had landed.

The first impressions of Iran were not enhanced by our taxi ride from the airport, chased for a few miles by a pack of more than fifty wild dogs - this at four o'clock in the morning. However the oasis of the new Hilton Hotel eventually provided suitable succour for two weary travellers.

Our first appointment, of many, with John Scott, the General Manager of Shellcott, was not until the afternoon. We therefore hired a taxi for a short sightseeing tour of Tehran. Within our first twenty-four hours in Tehran we were to witness eight traffic accidents, mainly because red traffic lights were considered a challenge by Iranian drivers. Fortunately during the day these collisions caused only vehicular damage since the grid-locked traffic restricted the speed of these Kamikaze drivers: we discovered it was only during the night, with lighter traffic, that motorists managed suicide as they drove at speed through red lights.

In those days most women wore the all-enveloping chador, but certainly not for political or religious reasons. The heat and the traffic pollution was so bad at mid-day that the chador, many brightly coloured and not the uniform black of today, was worn as protective covering. When they blew open in the wind it was to reveal, more frequently than not, the shortest of mini skirts.

Shellcott was an interesting concept being an amalgam of Shell Petroleum and Mitchell Cotts which operated agricultural projects worldwide. At that time the ambition of His Imperial Majesty Mohammed Reza Shah Pahlavi, Aryamehr, Shahanshah of Iran (or the Shah as I will henceforth call him) was for his nation to become self-sufficient in food. Thus any companies which wished to set up any operations in Iran always hedged their proposals with some agricultural project, however remotely connected, to gain the Shah's ear and subsequently his approval.

Thus it was that in 1970, with the pressures of the commercial and political aspirations of Shell, that Shellcott took over 37,500 acres of land near Shiraz with the intention of producing alfalfa (lucerne), sorghum and cotton.

Unfortunately, since it was only six years since the Shah's 1964 White Revolution when virtually all Iranian land had been taken away from the feudal landowners and distributed amongst the peasants, this move by Shellcott to dispossess nearly three thousand recently established "farmers" was not popular among the locals. The government built concrete shanty towns to house those who had lost their newly acquired land but failed to provide work for them. The Shellcott operations employed, on a fairly irregular basis, only about five hundred of these erstwhile farmers, leaving 2,500 very disaffected locals. This resulted initially with sabotage of both the crops and the equipment, but after a couple of visits by Savak, the Shah's brutal secret police, and the disappearance of the ringleaders an uneasy peace ensued. Savak had been established by the Shah in 1957 with the aid of the USA's CIA and Israel's Mossad.

Technically the whole Shellcott operation was flawed since it depended upon first levelling the land to a fall of only one centimetre in fifty metres; this required so many passes of massive levelling machines that much of the soil structure was destroyed, making the soil prone to capping with subsequent poor crop growth. All this David and I quickly realised on our visit to their Dezful farms.

In Tehran, before the conference started, we met a number of influential expatriates and nationals largely thanks to the Matthews Wrightson Middle Eastern negotiator, Philip Woods, whose life, following his career in British naval intelligence, had mainly been spent in the Middle East, particularly Iraq.

Among those we met before the Investment Conference was Saifi Khan Sadry, the archetypal "Mr Fix-it" in all fields: my notes at the time suggest that "Saifi's honesty is of a discretionary variety and certainly does not extend to government regulations". He assured us that additional technical assistance, or graft to put it bluntly, would amount to no more than 1½ per cent of our costs.

Of similar stature was Saifi's colleague, Sharpour Shakalili, with, if possible, even more dubious morality: his family descended from the dynasty of the previous Shah who was deposed by Reza Shah Pahlavi in 1925, entirely thanks to British machinations.

Ironically during our Iran visit the Shah made a television appearance denouncing corruption and admitting that he knew that many government and local officials had a special drawer in their offices for their "private rake-offs" but that he, the Shah and his officials, were going to stop this. "But Rome was not built in a day and my people must have patience…..."

In complete contrast were our other contacts: Charles Lister, Shell's fixer, due to retire in two months after a lifetime in the Middle East: Dr Owen Price, Director of the World Bank in Iran, and his assistant Australian Dennis Purcell; also many of our later contacts all of whom were genuinely seeking the best for Iran with complete integrity.

Between our meetings we walked through the crowded streets, avoiding treading into the often flooding, gullies alongside the pavements which were running with polluted water. Tehran was remembered by many British servicemen during the Second World War as a pleasant haven, a lovely city for rest and recuperation from the rigours of war, a city with only 400,000 inhabitants. By the time of our visit, only 25 years later, it had grown to four million people and there were still no underground sewers.

Avenue Fedozy was memorable because every shop traded either in gold or in carpets. Both these products were tempting, for beautifully crafted gold jewellery was sold by weight, the price decided by that day's London price-fix. Iranians consider it bad luck to buy old carpets, thus there were many second-hand bargains to be had.

On Monday 26 November 1973 all the delegates were pleased to be leaving the air polluted city of Tehran on a private charter plane, carrying all the sixty UK delegates to the Conference. At the end of the one hour flight to Shiraz we were taken by coaches, escorted by police in cars and on motor-cycles, sirens screaming, to the recently built Darius Hotel at Perspolis, or

Takht-e-Jamshîd to give it its correct Persian name. En route, surprisingly, there was only one road accident involving one of the delegate coaches and a police car.

This modern hotel had been built to accommodate the delegates to the 2500 years' celebration of the Shah in 1971 and was a classic example of good management, at least while we were there. We were confronted in reception by three huge ice swans carrying heaps of the best Caspian caviar. This dish was available throughout the day – and night. One began to believe that it was the staple diet of the locals. Indeed every time I left Iran I sensibly carried with me at least one kilogramme of the best canned caviar.

The midday outside temperature in Perspolis, even in late November, was at least 70° Fahrenheit whilst at night it was well below freezing because, away from the coast, the whole central area of Iran is at least 5,000 feet high. In spite of this daytime heat, the ornamental pools at the hotel remained frozen all day.

Whilst we were in Iran the British fuel shortage was just beginning as a result of the Yom Kippur war in the Middle East. When Peter Walker (later Lord Walker), then the British Minister for Trade and Industry, presented his conference speech his opening gambit was to suggest that the excessive central heating in the conference room should be turned down and the fuel saved should be sent to Britain.

As it became clearer that the major topic for the Iranians was agriculture and the opportunities for investment in Iran in this field, there was an overt sense of dismay by the British industrialists present that this was a wasted journey for them as they knew little, and cared even less, about food production.

Lord Stokes, of Leyland fame, sitting next to me at the alphabetically seated conference, complained bitterly that as a young salesman forty years earlier he had spent time selling tractors to the Iranians but had no intention of becoming

99

involved in agriculture ever again. Lords Jellico and Nelson were equally disgruntled at the way in which the conference was based on agriculture. Since David and I were the only British delegates who had the slightest idea of farming it fell upon us to lead many of the discussions.

The Iranian Government, immediately prior to the conference, had published its latest Five Year Plan, in which about 90 per cent of the nation's income was expected to come from petroleum sales. Just as the conference started the world price of oil went berserk, rising to three times its pre-Yom Kippur war level. Thus the Iranian economists worked through the nights to update the Five Year Plan. Naively all they did was to multiply their national income by 290 per cent.

I did ask Iranian Minister of Agriculture Rouhani whether he did not think that the virtual trebling of oil prices might have an adverse effect on the cost of the nation's imports? My suggestion was ignored and the modified Plan was put forward as the way Iran thought their Five Year Plan would operate.

One of the outstanding speakers at the Conference was His Excellency Mehdi Samii, the powerful president of the Iranian Agricultural Development Fund, a real gentleman and strangely leader of the opposition in Parliament. We were to obtain a great deal of help and co-operation from Mehdi in setting up our farming enterprises.

During the conference David and I went with the leading Iranian agriculturist present, Iraj Hedayat, to his property, less than one hour's drive north of Shiraz.. This impressive operation consisted of three thousand acres of intensive food production, all irrigated by water bursting out of a spring in the middle of his farm. Iraj had made a wonderful oasis around the source of the spring with lawns and weeping willow trees.

His major crop was tomatoes which were canned on site in one of the most modern canning factories outside Britain and the USA, both countries with whom he dealt.

Iraj, later to become our close friend and farming partner, had been educated at Loughborough College: indeed he had played full-back for the winning Loughborough rugby team in one of the London Sevens' championships.

Iraj was a fervent Iranian patriot, in the best sense of the word. One day, whilst I was with him, he received an offer from an American university of $4 million for his unique collection of ancient Persian glass. He declined saying that he would, on his death, donate his collection to the Museum of Iran in Tehran.

The conference at Perspolis continued with exhortations from the Iranian ministers present for British investment, especially in food production areas. The Prime Minister, Amir Hovayda, who always wore a home grown orchid in his lapel, was especially friendly, presumably once Iraj Hedayat had vouched privately for our agricultural expertise and genuine interest.

All the conference delegates were taken to visit the ruins of the ancient capital of Persia, now known as Persepolis, meaning in Greek, City of Persians. The Persians had called the city Persa during the rule of Darius around 500 BC. Darius had made Persepolis the new capital of his kingdom, replacing Pasargadae. Its grandeur had gradually faded, though it survived the changes of many dynasties, in spite of being pillaged from time to time by various invading hoards. With the coming of the 3rd century AD, and the Sasanid Empire, Persepolis was deprived of its importance forever. Modern excavations started in 1931 and these are probably the finest ruins to be found in Iran.

The finale of the conference was a banquet held in the Tented City, built, like the Darius Hotel, to entertain the international guests attending the 2500 year celebrations two years earlier. During dinner the air-conditioning plant failed and the tented room became colder and colder until, after about an hour, repairs were effected. At one stage the Iranian Prime Minister stood up and announced that although some of us believed that the air-conditioning had gone wrong, it hadn't. The hosts, he said, were deliberately acclimatising the British delegates to conditions to which they would be returning in England.

When the conference ended most delegates returned immediately to England: however David and I set off to see some more of the country. We flew the 250 miles north west to Isfahan, surely one of the most beautiful cities of the Middle East. There we stayed at the famous Shah Abbas hotel, recently built but designed in the ancient Safavid caravanserai style. Sadly this hotel was virtually destroyed by rioters at the start of the 1979 revolution which overthrew the Shah.

After two days looking at the very peasant oriented local farming we flew on to Ahwaz, a further 250 miles south. At the airport we had difficulty in hiring a taxi to drive us the ninety miles to the Shellcott farms at Dezful. The problem was that we had been told that everyone at Ahwaz knew the Shellcott operations and, even with us having no Farsi, the Iranian language, at all, every taxi driver would know the way. Ultimately, after much gesticulating and poring over maps, one driver insinuated that indeed he knew exactly where we wanted to go.

Full of confidence we set off on the supposed two hour journey northwards. After one hour we reached a major y-junction, at which the driver turned around and asked us which way he should go. After studying the very poor sketch map and the angle of the sun, and the time of day and the date, we opted for the one heading more nearly north.

Our self congratulations knew no bounds when, after another half-an-hour of steady motoring over the rough road we came to a signpost to the town of Dez; later we were to learn that at that point we had been very close to Shellcott. When we finally did reach Dez the local police indeed knew the Shellcott farms and pointed out the correct route, back along the way we had come but with better directions. Thus it was that our planned ninety mile two hour journey actually took six hours and covered more than 150 most uncomfortable miles.

Ian Davenport, the resident Shellcott manager, and his wife Diane, were most understanding and hospitable and insisted that, after we had seen the farm, it would be far too late to return to Ahwaz and that we should stay the night, an invitation we gladly accepted. Ian suggested that on our way back we should take the ferry across the river we would have to cross on our shortest route to Ahwaz. In response to my question, he did not think that it would be necessary to reserve a place on the ferry at this time of the year. Later we appreciated why.

The thirteen thousand acres currently under production had all been laser-levelled and the soil was extremely unstable due to the many passes of heavy earth moving equipment. However the day-to-day management was impressive in spite of the Shellcott concept that experts in London could decide on cropping and even control local management decisions on a daily basis. They were convinced that large scale broad-acre farming was the right course for them and dismissed a later proposal from us to grow tomatoes for Yek-o-Yek, Iraj Hedayat's canning company. Local expatriate managers were earning a little under £5,000 a year, including a 75 per cent overseas allowance: of course housing and travel were provided by the company. It was a hard life for expatriates since it was difficult to understand the local ways.

After a most convivial evening and very comfortable night, our driver, to our surprise, appeared at the due time and Ian, in his Toyota Landcruiser led us to the ferry. There it became obvious why it had not been necessary to book a place: the ferry consisted of a fifteen foot by ten foot wooden planked platform strapped to forty-five gallon oil drums: the method of propulsion was by pulling oneself along the overhead cable. After much persuasion we convinced our driver that this precarious contraption would transport his precious car and thus, luckily without mishap, we crossed the river and arrived at Ahwaz airport in less than two hours. After a one and a half hour flight for the 500 miles to Tehran: we arrived at the Semiramis, a typical Iranian hotel.

We spent the Saturday and Sunday locally around Tehran. We had numerous meetings (for these were normal working days, Friday being the 'Sunday' in Iran) in the city, including one in the British Embassy, where we were welcomed by the Ambassador Sir Peter Ramsbotham, an outstanding diplomat doing a great deal to further Anglo-Iran relations: he was later to become HM Ambassador to Washington, only to be replaced in the middle of his posting when Prime Minister James Callahan nepotically appointed his then son-in-law to replace him. The only person to emerge from this reprehensible affair with dignity was Sir Peter.

We also met various Iranian government ministers and our local "fixers" and were welcomed warmly as possible agricultural investors and operators. Also, after reluctantly putting our lives in the hands of a taxi driver, we spent a fascinating few hours at the farm managed by expatriate Brit John Davies. Together with his wife Jean, he ran this Iranian owned 750 acre farm at Gazvine, some sixty miles west of Tehran, efficiently producing prodigious quantities of milk from 600 zero-grazed Holstein cows for the Tehran market. Jean ran the local medical welfare clinic. Having lived there for eight years they were able to provide us with much useful information about benefits and problems.

We also called at the El Al Airline offices in Tehran, outside which a bomb had exploded two months earlier. Sitting around the office were half a dozen young men, apparently students, casually dressed and reading paperbacks. On the Sunday night, 1 December 1973, after a prodigious search of our baggage, we took the 1300 mile flight to Tel Aviv. As we boarded the virtually empty El Al aircraft we noticed that the six "students" from the travel office were already dispersed throughout the cabin. When we disembarked at Tel Aviv the "students" did not disembark with us - obviously they were sky marshals.

Unusually for any immigration officials, and especially ones in Israel, we were greeted very warmly and considered almost as heroes to visit Israel so soon after the Yom Kippur war. Ironically as we drove our hire car from Tel Aviv to Haifa we were caught in a radar speed trap. However, the Israeli policemen said that although they needed the fines to pay for the war he would not fine us as we were the first tourists he had seen since the fighting.

We spent two delightful days with my old friend and colleague Professor Emmanuel Yalan and his wife, Judith, in Haifa. Emmanuel and David quickly built up a close rapport since the two of them were lateral thinkers and conceived way-out ideas, many of which were sound.

Visits to the Milout Cooperative, the Hahalal Moshav and Kibbutz Yifat, all leaders in their own fields, provided us with a wonderful overview of current Israeli agricultural thinking, which led the world with its innovative ideas and practices.

We arrived back in England at mid-day on Wednesday 5 December 1973 to be met by Dick Bridges, the Fountain Farming Chapmansford Farm foreman, in our petrol guzzling Range Rover. Paradoxically on the way home from the airport we were in dire need of petrol and I had the greatest difficulty in persuading the garage attendant to allow us a charitable two gallons. I think it was only my telling him that we had just flown in from Iran, where petrol was five pence a gallon to motorists - only one penny to farmers – that he generously allowed us this benefice.

David and I were completely convinced that there an important role for Fountain Farming in Iran and we both reported enthusiastically to our various masters. The summary of my long and detailed report to John Eldridge, Chairman of

Matthews Wrightson, and Nigel Dykhoff, Chairman of Fountain Farming was: *There is no doubt that the present intention of the Government of Iran is to encourage by all means possible a spectacular increase in its agricultural output. There is equally little doubt that Fountain Farming could and should play an important part in this developing situation.*

Our masters accepted our reasoning and following a visit to England by Iraj Hedayat, during which he met all those interested in furthering the cause of Fountain Farming in Iran, a decision was taken to take the project further. Thus in March 1974 David and I returned to meet Iraj in Tehran, flying direct with British Airways, a new daily flight to cater for the huge interest in Iran, thanks to their massive oil revenues.

The whole atmosphere within Tehran had changed, it was frenetic. Genuine business entrepreneurs and conmen were there in force. Even with Telexed confirmation, a room booking at the Hilton was worth nothing until a $50 bill had crossed the palm of the receptionists. Even the swimming pool huts were being rented to visitors and all the conference rooms were let, dormitory style. Fortunately for us the Park Hotel, a city central hotel, was owned by a great friend of Iraj and so our bookings were sacrosanct. Perhaps it helped that I always took out with me a whole Stilton cheese, triple wrapped in aluminium foil, as a gift to the owner?

One place that did not change, except the extra difficulty of obtaining a table, was Leon's restaurant. Our first dinner on every visit to Tehran was to this superb eatery owned and run by White Russian expatriates: starting with Russian Borscht followed by blinis and caviar – one knew that there could be a future!

Now the problem was to find the land on which to start our Iranian farming. We had already determined that we were not going to follow the Shellcott concept of a massive, London run, industrialized farming operation, employing relatively few local workers.

We were looking for land to provide an initial base from which we could expand a profitable farming enterprise. Our intention was to start with one expatriate manager but to employ Iranian agricultural college graduates to be trained on our British farms before taking over our anticipated expanding operations in Iran. So a number of exploratory trips to Iran followed, each one usually of about ten days.

After a meeting with Agricultural Minister Rouhani in Tehran on 28th April 1974, we were offered a vast acreage of reputedly superb quality land on the border with Soviet Armenia at Makou. Thus it was that Iraj, David and I flew on the very efficient Iran Air flight to Tabriz in north east Iran.

Incidentally Iran Air had a simple procedure for discouraging "no-shows". If you changed your flight ticket more than three days before the flight there was a nominal charge of £5. If you changed between then and twenty-fours you paid 25 per cent of the fare; within twenty-four hours of the flight you lost your ticket; there were few "no-shows" and thus no need for over-booking.

From there we were driven to Makou to discover that the land was on the border with the Soviet Union, separated only by the majestic Telyhakiya Gory River. It bode well that the Soviet side was covered with an abundance of intensive superbly managed horticultural crops. As I took photographs of the Soviet land, including the closely spaced watch towers, all manned by binocular toting soldiers, both David and Iraj moved further away from me. Much to our delight the observers simply waved at us, rather than any alternative.

We dug deep holes at frequent intervals over vast areas of this unused Iranian land and found the soil was ideal for intensive vegetable production and the river would have provided more than enough water for irrigation, but we were perplexed as to why it lay apparently unutilised.

That evening whilst we enjoyed dinner in the local hostelry Iraj explained to the locals the presence of the two foreigners with him. It turned out that the local Bakhtiari tribe had, for the past many thousands of years, driven their huge flocks of sheep, totalling about six million head, through the area in which we were interested in farming whilst travelling to and from their upland grazing. They grazed their sheep on the lowlands during the winter and the uplands during the summer, taking up to six weeks to transfer their flocks. This bi-annual migration we felt would be, to put it at its mildest, a disincentive to taking over this tract of land for intensive vegetable farming.

The next day we flew the very short distance from Tabriz to Rezaiyeh across the lake. The Scots pilot kept the Iran Air Boeing 727 jet well below one thousand feet as he announced that this would give us all a good view of the lake, true. Then back to Tehran.

On reporting to Minister Rouhani that although we thought the land was perfect the tribal needs would rather inhibit our production of vegetables. Rouhani, basically a brilliant engineer who designed many of the vast dams in Iran, said that this should not worry us as he would get them to take their sheep a different way – an unlikely tale. Thus our search for land continued.

Incidentally, Minister Rouhani, soon after he came to office realised that the first large scale dairying operations, financed and managed by overseas companies, and stocked with imported Holstein cows, were producing very much more milk than were the local cows. He therefore proposed the slaughter of the entire indigenous dairy herds: fortunately sanity prevailed. Everything in Iran had to be seen to be on a huge scale and in full operation immediately. Instant food production was the somewhat mythical objective.

The Minister had recently sanctioned the building of a sheep complex near Shiraz which would house more than a million head. There was a slight problem in that no one had considered from where the considerable quantities of feed were going to be produced to feed the sheep nor how they would get rid of the sheep dung. We declined the opportunity of taking on the management of this unusual enterprise - I assured the Minister that we did not have the necessary expertise.

The next area for seeking suitable land was in the south east of the country. Iraj's driver had set off in his Land Rover a day earlier to drive the 400 miles from Shiraz to Bandar Abbas where this would be his first ever view of an ocean. He met us at Bandar Abbas airport, situated on the Persian Gulf coast. That day we drove the short distance of eighty miles to Rudan; here there was a high plateau completely surrounded by hills growing tomatoes for export shipment to other gulf states. The temperature in this 6,000 acre area was reputed never to have dropped below 70° F, day or night, winter or summer. The whole operation was remarkably primitive. Ripe tomatoes were picked by hand into 40 pound capacity wooden crates: the crates were then dragged across the field to be stacked in full sun to await the lorry to deliver them to the docks in Bandar Abbas. There they waited on the dockside to be loaded into junks which took them out to the lighters moored offshore, for onward delivery to Bahrain, Qatar, UAE and other Gulf countries. We surmised that less than twenty per cent of the picked fruit would reach its destination in edible condition. Sadly the landowner wanted far too high a rent to make a business proposition worthwhile.

The next day we set off in the Land Rover for a four hundred mile epic drive, in temperatures which exceeded one hundred and twenty degrees Fahrenheit, in a Land Rover which was not air-conditioned. It was a further twelve months before we exported suitably air-conditioned Range Rovers into Iran. Our journey took us through the Jiroft desert where we stopped for lunch at an amazing man made oasis. Inside the stone walls were thirty acres, growing every crop imaginable, surrounding a spectacular house.

The irrigation pump for the myriad of crops was fixed outside a beautifully tiled bath house; cold water from a deep aquifer was pumped into the deep tiled bath, from whence it flowed to the fields for crop irrigation. I was invited to jump in, which I did - fully clothed. I then stripped off and hung my now dustless clothes on a convenient line in the sun; I wallowed in the bath for about fifteen minutes and then climbed out to dress in my now once more clean and dry clothes.

At the villa we were entertained to a magnificent lunch by the owner, whose family had known the Hedayats for generations. There was no sign of any females. The owner had been a close collaborator with Doctor Mossadegh, Prime Minister of Iran from 1951 until he was overthrown by a British and American inspired coup in 1953. Thus he had been exiled by the Shah. Later I asked Iraj why he lived alone and was amazed to be told that his wife and daughters, some of whom were married, lived there but would never appear in front of faranges, or foreigners. Later that day we stopped for tea where the farm manager was married to a Scots girl; we did not see her either although she was there and had prepared tea for us, complete with Scottish oatcakes.

After a long and very tiring day we finally reached our overnight stop. There the news had reached the village that "Prince" Iraj Hedayat would be staying overnight with two farange friends. The village had built a remarkable double walled grass hut, about twenty feet square and fifteen feet high, especially for our use. Around this was a water filled moat and two men were bucketing the water on to the hut. The temperature outside was in excess of a hundred degrees, inside it was a most pleasant seventy. The floor was covered by a beautiful Persian carpet and there were various drinks available for us, all of course non-alcoholic And there were three camp beds carefully made up.

After a shower we saw that a carpet had been laid a few yards from our hut and a gigantic meal was laid out for us. I ate very little as I had been suffering from a severe stomach upset, not unusual for visitors to Iran until one realised that all ice was contaminated.

The following morning as we drove out of the village compound we passed a much smaller grass hut, not far from our larger one. Iraj explained that this had been prepared for the village maiden to entertain the faranges but Iraj had felt that we were in no fit state to do justice to England – I think he was joking?

Then it was on to Kerman, a city overflowing with antiquities including such wonders as the Jabal-i-Sang, meaning the *Mountain of Stone*: this domed chamber is one of the most amazing monuments of southern Iran and one of the most puzzling. Neither its exact date nor use is known, only that it dates from the late 12th century and was possibly never finished.

Then on to Yazd, reputedly where homosexuals were allowed to "marry". I was wearing my usual shorts and long socks and as we climbed out of the Land Rover Iraj alarmed me by saying that it was only the homosexuals who wore shorts in Yazd, "but that's fine as I haven't seen a good fight for years"! As I walked through the bazaars I was chatted up by all and sundry, including a uniformed policeman, but no fights developed. We saw the magnificent Sky Light at Dowlatabad Gardens' and the dome of the Jamea Mosque.

From here we drove to Isfahan to take the return flight to Tehran having decided that we had not seen any suitable land that was available for our proposed enterprise. So we returned to England and the relative ease of running a 30,000 acre farming operation in more familiar surroundings.

However the lure of Iran still lingered and Iraj, now married to Ferrie Fedayoun, came over to England on his honeymoon. He had heard of a possible property suitable for us in the north east of the country and he knew the owner who was keen for us to take it on and develop it for intensive farming.

So once more David and I flew to Tehran and then, after meeting the landowner in Tehran, our next flight was to the Holy City of Mashad, in the north east of the country, a city which received more pilgrims every year than did Saudi Arabia's Mecca. It also boasted an Inter-Continental Hotel which was superbly managed by an Israeli. In those days the Israelis were very active in Iran and indeed most of Iran's agricultural expertise was provided by Israelis. We visited the Gawhar Shad mosque before going on the short distance to Torbat-e-Jam, towards the Afghan border and the possible land.

We saw prolific numbers of the underground qanats, (aquifers or kariz in Farsi), mostly built between 800 and 500 BC and still in near perfect condition. There existed about two thousand five hundred miles of these underground tunnels used for bringing the plentiful water from the mountains to irrigate the arable and grazing lands. The tunnels are mainly semi-circular, either bricked or dug out of solid rock, and they are about ten feet high. It makes one humble to recall what the Ancient Brits were doing (had we even invented woad?) all that time ago when the Persians were digging this sophisticated underground complex.

The land we were being offered to rent consisted of 6,500 acres of good quality soil, capable of growing a wide range of crops, including intensive vegetables. The quanats serving the property were in perfect condition and would provide ample water for irrigating the whole farm, after installing eight pumping stations. Also included, in the town of Torbat-e-Jam, was a first class house suitable for an expatriate manager. We also understood that ample local labour would be available.

Iraj had assured us, and we were later to discover for ourselves, that Iranian workers are unlike those in most developing countries in that they are extremely proud of what they do and how they do it. Even though most were illiterate, we were to learn that if you gave an Iranian employee a new tractor he would use it to its best capability and a year later it would still look as though it had just come from the showroom. This pride extended to the crops themselves as I was to learn later. We spent two days digging holes and generally checking the soil and the topography against the rather basic map available. When we later returned to England we were laden down with copious amounts of soil samples for analysis at the Ministry laboratories at Reading. The scientists there were fascinated by the unusual soils and we had to admit to their origin.

On our return to Tehran, at a very amicable and social meeting with the absentee owner, we quickly agreed the terms of the lease, which was to be for ten years with us having an option to renew. He told us that his brother, the then Iranian ambassador to London, would probably lease us his neighbouring farm of similar size. Sadly this did not happen since the ambassador was a very keen gambler and after having his gambling debts paid off by the Shah foolishly he continued to gamble. After his next losses, which we understood reached another one million pounds (again paid by the Shah), he died falling off (?) the balcony of his London flat and his farm was expropriated by the Shah. Iraj came in with us as a partner and this gave us an even better market for some of our produce through his nationally known canning company Yek-o-Yek (One and One).

Obviously if we were going to farm this land intensively we needed workers and equipment. We quickly managed to employ 125 excellent full time workers, male and female, and the new farm tackle followed rapidly. During harvest time we employed a further 350 workers.

The pumping of the water from the qanats was more problematic. We could use either massive new diesel pumps or electricity from the overhead mains grid. Against our better judgement, but influenced by the considerable saving in capital cost and running expenses of using electric pumps rather than diesel we used electricity, having been told by Minister Rouhani that if we used electricity it would provide the excuse to upgrade the local power supplier and that at all times we would be guaranteed a continuous supply as priority users. We were later to rue this decision.

The next task was to find a manager with considerable expatriate experience. After many weeks of interviewing applicants we selected Roger Lough, a New Zealander who was an Australian graduate but currently was heading the agricultural department of the Zambian Development Bank in Lusaka. A good choice, for he found that the capabilities of the local workers far exceeded anything he had come upon in other developing countries. Only half-jokingly he included Australia under this heading.

Within twelve months we were growing a variety of vegetables, including nearly a thousand acres of Kharbuseh melons, unique to Iran, a crisp greenish colour and with a high sugar content. The only hurdle for marketing these in new areas would be that they were huge and looked exactly like very large marrows. They were so firm that they could be stored up to five feet deep and would keep in perfect condition for many months.

When we exported them to England by air freight, our idea was that they should be cut in half, sealed in cling-film, and a one inch section should be made available to the consumer for tasting to educate people to their unique taste. During the mid-seventies cargo planes were flying in to Iran loaded but seldom were the carriers able to find return loads, thus air freight from Iran was ridiculously cheap.

The farm, Sherkate Sahami Landkesht, straddled the only road that ran from Mashad to Afghanistan, which at that time was a popular hippie trail. The Iranian border guards inspected the hippie vehicles coming across from Afghanistan in a most cursory fashion. Thus lulled into a false sense of security by the time they reached Torbet-e-Jam, they had taken their caches of drugs out of their hiding places and were happily smoking pot.

However between Torbat-e-Jam and Mashad there was a permanent police post and every vehicle was stopped and most were searched. The Iranians had an uncomplicated system of dealing with those caught carrying drugs: if they had a small amount, sufficient in the opinion of the police to be purely for their own use, they were put straight into Mashad jail for five years. If, however, the police considered they were trading then they shot them on the spot, burying the bodies locally and selling off the vehicles for "police funds". I am afraid that a lot of hippies disappeared in this manner.

One Friday (the Iranian day off) David Rushton, Roger Lough and I took the farm driver and went to look at some new land which we had been offered, even closer to the Afghan border. When we reached the hill top village of Salishabad we were arrested by the military police "for having crossed illegally from Afghanistan" and taken before the guard commander, an artillery captain who greeted us clad in singlet and underpants. He spoke excellent English and welcomed us warmly, pulling out an unopened bottle of Johnny Walker whisky which he insisted we shared with him while his signaller contacted his headquarters in Tehran to check on our bonafides.

So there we were, on an Iranian holy day, a couple of miles from the Afghan border, three of us awaiting validation from Tehran by military radio. David, born in Burma and who did not see a wheel until he fled with his missionary parents in an overloaded Dakota to get away before the Japanese occupation: Roger, a New Zealander with an Australian passport and an address in

115

Zambia; and me, relatively straightforward, at least compared with the others.

Once I had confessed to having once being a captain too in the British Royal Artillery, an army pilot to boot, the hospitality grew even more extravagant. It is true that the Iranians adhere to the belief that the host is the prisoner of their guests.

At the behest of the captain the villagers laid out a huge Persian carpet in the village square and soon we were tucking in to a feast. After lunch the captain disappeared back to his quarters leaving us to be entertained by the villagers and his lieutenant.

I had explained to the lieutenant that if we could not leave by three o'clock we would have to stay the night as it would be too dangerous for our driver in the hills after dark. Thus at three o'clock precisely the lieutenant gave us permission to depart.

As we were heading down the hill a shot rang out and a bullet kicked up the stones in front of the car; looking up we saw the lieutenant gesticulating madly for us to return. Very reluctantly we did, there to be taken in to the now fully uniformed captain's quarters. We feared the worst as he commanded us to sit. But smiling broadly he informed us that we could not leave – until the bottle of Johnny Walker was empty. From then on I knew no more until waking up the next morning in our farm house in Tobat-e-Jam.

David and I flew back to Tehran for more meetings with ministers and His Excellency Mehdi Samii, a true gentleman and friend and the powerful president of the Iranian Agricultural Development Fund. We were now 'blue eyed boys' in official eyes as we had in record time set up an efficient food producing operation employing a considerable number of locals, and we had dispossessed no one.

In our initial negotiations in 1973 and 1974 we had found the British Embassy, under Sir Peter Ramsbotham, to be of great help, furthering and easing our discussions. This changed dramatically when Sir Peter was promoted to the post of ambassador to Washington. The whole attitude of the Embassy changed and we were considered but one of many UK companies demanding what they considered to be unreasonable help from the hard-worked Embassy staff. This really did inhibit many of our discussions with Iranian ministers. On one occasion we organised a reception for many of those involved in Iranian politics, especially those connected with agriculture and the land. Two senior ministers appeared on time, together with half a dozen junior ministers. The British Embassy representative staggered in, literally, just as our last Iranian guest was leaving: the offender shall be nameless, having gone on to ambassadorial status later.

Coincidentally the 75 Club (see Appendix) was entertaining the Rt Hon Michael Heseltine, then in opposition, to lunch at Quaglino's on 29th June 1976. As a result of considerable problems with the Foreign Office about the Tehran British Embassy I arrived late for the lunch, after our guest. I apologised and said that it was really thanks to our diplomats that I had committed this discourtesy. He was interested and offered to take me back to the House of Commons after lunch and see what he could do to help.

Interestingly after lunch at which Michael Heseltine performed brilliantly we were trying to find a taxi in Jermyn Street. Suddenly a Jaguar stopped, the driver, being a fan of Heseltine, offered to drive him anywhere. Would this happen today, thirty years later?

When we arrived at the House Heseltine was met by his personal secretary who reminded him that he had not finished an important speech which he had to present that evening. Heseltine said that he was not to be disturbed for half an hour, during this time he was obviously successful in twisting some Embassy tails in Tehran, as when I arrived on the Tehran Embassy doorstep forty eight hours later I was treated like a VIP.

I had been invited by Minister Rouhani to suggest ways in which his government could increase the number of imported dairy stock coming into the country. I suggested a transport subsidy on dairy heifer calves, say up to six months old, from recognised Holstein breeders. My idea of limiting this to calves was firstly that these animals would then have eighteen months to acclimatise themselves to the vastly different conditions they would experience before they calved down at two years old. Secondly it was possible to fit a greater number of calves than older stock into a jumbo cargo plane. However when Minster Ruahani realised that this would not increase the numbers actually milking for at least another two years he modified my plan. The 100 per cent air freight subsidy was limited to in-calf cows and heifers due to calve within four months of landing in Iran. This was absurd on every count, even for short term short sighted political expediency. Many of these valuable animals thus imported aborted, some died, and virtually none became acclimatised.

At this time the chemical giant ICI was trying to persuade the Iranians that ICI should be given permission to build a polymer plant in Iran. They realised that if they simultaneously proposed setting up an agricultural project then their polymer plant application would be considered more rapidly and certainly more favourably.

They sought my help and I proposed, and designed, a five hundred cow dairy unit for them, using a rotary milking parlour with fifty standings. When this was submitted to the Minister he told them it was not large enough. The simple solution was to build a second, mirror image unit adjoining, thus milking one thousand cows. This too was rejected as being insignificant, in spite of pointing out that there were no dairy herds in Britain of even five hundred cows.

So, really with tongue in cheek and against my advice, ICI submitted plans for three such back-to-back units milking three thousand cows. This too was rejected by Minster Ruahani who enquired as to what was the size of the biggest dairy herd in the world: on learning that the Alta Dena dairy in California milked seventeen thousand cows he insisted that Iran wanted one bigger than this. Even ICI were then convinced of the absurdity of the proposition and did not take it further. Whether the ICI polymer plant was built I know not.

On returning to our farm I was delighted with the enthusiasm and skills of our employees at Sherkate Sahami Landkesht and the crops looked really first class. Roger Louth had a good rapport with his employees although his domestic arrangements were far from ideal. Because of there being no international schools available near the farm, not even in Mashad, for his two teenage children, Roger's family lived in Tehran while he flew back there most weekends to be with them after spending the weekdays on the farm.

On one visit to the new ambassador, Sir Anthony Parsons, I enquired as to the chances of setting up an English school at Mashad. He carefully opened his large ledger listing the names and addresses of all the British residents in Iran. He discovered that there were five in Mashad but, as he put it "not much use to us as they are all in jail there". Long before we resolved this domestic dilemma the Shah had "departed Iran on holiday".

The farms' irrigation requirement was colossal with eight electric pumps running continuously. During the summer months we needed about a quarter of a million gallons per cropped acre, or a grand total in excess of a billion gallons or about one million gallons per pump per day – a great deal of electricity was required but, as Minster Ruahani assured me, once again, at a meeting in Tehran at the beginning of July, that we were priority users and were guaranteed a continuous supply. I returned home full of confidence - sadly to be short lived.

119

Two days after arriving home I had an urgent call from Roger Lough: we were being limited to only five hours of electricity a day. This spelt certain disaster as in temperatures frequently above one hundred degrees non-irrigated crops would rapidly burn up. I immediately telephoned both the Foreign Office in London and then, since they were of no help, the British Embassy in Tehran who were of little use either. I did get through on the telephone to Reza Doroudian, Under Secretary at the Ministry of Co-operation and Rural Affairs, who I had met on an earlier visit when I had been impressed by his youthful enthusiasm. He promised to brief Minster Ruahani.

Unfortunately Iraj was away in the USA at the time, and so the next day I arrived in Tehran and asked the British Embassy to accompany me to see Minster Ruahani. Unfortunately this was too short a notice for them so I was alone when I saw Minster Ruahani, together with his deputy Reza Douroudian, who had already briefed the minister. He knew about the problem and was full of apology, it was all a big mistake and of course we were priority users and would have electricity all the time. To prove it he had organised for me to fly to Mashad that evening to see for myself that all was now in order and that the pumps were once again working full time.

This was my most emotionally moving visit to the farm for I was greeted by a group of our Iranian foremen who tearfully told me of their worries of what was going to happen to "their" crops if we were limited in our electricity supplies. By the time of my arrival full supply had been restored and minimum damage had been done to our crops. These Iranians, mainly illiterate, were typical examples of the best of Iran, loyalty was their watchword.

The electricity "post mortem" highlighted once again the corruption that was endemic amongst even minor officials and the local electricity company manager, apparently being disappointed at not receiving any backhanders from us, was "interviewed" by Savak and disappeared from the region. We had no further problems with either the electricity or the hard working pumps.

Prior to 1976 it is generally accepted that the Shah had underwritten the Kurdish disturbances in Iraq since he was determined that it would be Tehran not Baghdad which was accepted as the financial capital of the Middle East. That year the Shah came to terms with the Iraqi government and ceased to finance the dissident Kurds.

Three thousand of the Kurdish warriors were exiled and billeted on Iraj's farm near Shiraz. Iraj and I spent one evening with these remarkable men. It was only too apparent that their whole lives had been spent, most agreeably, in either warring or whoring. It was clear, even to me, that there would never be peace in Kurdistan until these people had their own autonomous country.

At that time the import duty into Iran on new vehicles was 350 percent, which made imports economically impractical. However the Shah was so impressed by the Range Rover that he decided that he wanted fifty for his Pahlavi Foundation. He thus reduced, for a period of six months only, the import duty to fifty per cent, specifically for off-road vehicles.

When I returned to England I was amazed to discover that British Leyland, the manufacturers of the Range Rover knew nothing of this. What a lost opportunity, again, by Leyland. Every time I had flown to Iran I had carried half a dozen oil filters and also fan belts for Land Rovers, these items always in short supply from Leyland dealers there.

We decided that we would export two Range Rovers, one for Iraj and one for the farm. I collected the first one from the Basingstoke Rover dealers, complete with an air conditioning unit attached to the roof: Leyland had yet to equip their export vehicles with air-conditioning, thus losing out to the fully equipped Toyota Landcruiser.

Once I had driven this air-conditioned vehicle around England for the then necessary one thousand miles running-in period I determined that I would always have air-con in my car. After its first service, and the correction of a few minor faults, my elder son, Andrew aged 21, with a friend, then set off to drive the vehicle to Tehran. Andrew had already driven this route once before, also in a Range Rover, as part of a Charterhouse school expedition, thus he, at least, knew the way. In Istanbul the Range Rover was pillaged and their luggage stolen, unfortunately including Andrew's spare pair of glasses, thus he was left with only his contact lenses, without which he was very short-sighted.

When they arrived at Karaj they called in at the Jean and John Davis farm for a welcome break where Andrew lost both his contact lenses when he unthinkingly dived into their swimming pool. The Davises did not hesitate; they drained the pool through muslin and found both of them, much to Andrew's relief thus enabling him to drive on to Tehran.

There was a further problem for when Andrew entered Iran from Turkey his passport was marked with the vehicle number and a declaration that he had to take the vehicle out with him when he left Iran, or else pay import duty. This potential bureaucratic nightmare was solved by Andrew and his friend hitching a lift home on one of the British cattle carrying cargo aircraft flying empty home to Stansted: passports were not required by the crew!

The Shah failed to persuade Leyland to let him have his fifty Range Rovers within the time period and so virtually all the vehicles imported by the Pahlavi Foundation during the six months tax semi-moratorium were Toyota Landcruisers.

We continued to farm at Sherkate Sahami Landkesht for another two and a half years producing melons, tomatoes and distinctive small cucumbers with great success. This continued until His Imperial Majesty Mohammed Reza Shah Pahlavi, Aryamehr,

Shahanshah of Iran, was massively misadvised by both the British and American governments thus allowing the disaffected revolutionaries of the nation free rein.

I watched from England the sad, and so unnecessary, disintegration of the Iranian nation, regretting that in spite of all the obsequious behaviour of both British and American governments we did nothing to help prevent the débacle, although I am certain that we really only meant to teach the Shah a lesson and make it plain that we thought he was becoming too self-important.

My experience in Iran was one of the most interesting chapters of my life and I felt that history would show that the Shah did considerably more good for his nation than harm. The Shah had for instance decreed early in the 1970s that every child over the age of six should go to school and instigated incentives to achieve this admirable objective.

When children arrived at school they were given a high-protein biscuit and a glass of reconstituted dried milk; in addition they were each given a small sealed tin containing rice, meat, vegetables and gravy; and before leaving for home they would heat these cans and eat the contents in their classrooms - a large portion of these foodstuffs were produced by Yek-o-Yek. Thus every child who attended school had a fully balanced daily diet. Another law was passed by the Shah forbidding the use of children younger than twelve in carpet making.

Once it became obvious that the Shah had departed forever Iraj sent his wife and two children, together with his house staff, to England, there to await events.

Early in 1978 Iraj had been appointed chief agricultural advisor to the Shah to try to bring some sanity into the vastly overblown schemes being dreamed up by the Shah's sycophantic ministers, all vying with each other to impress their ruler. This he was gradually, but very slowly, achieving.

When his family had left Iraj offered his agricultural expertise to the new powers for however much he disagreed with the revolution "I am Iranian, and my country needs me" was his view, expressed to me.

All was well for at least six months of the new regime and his expertise was much used, but as was the norm in that harrowing environment, he was suddenly arrested without charge and incarcerated in the dreaded Evin prison. Unlike most prisoners a price, normally a quarter of a million dollars, was not put on his head, and after two weeks he was unexpectedly released still without charge.

I spoke to him on the telephone from England after his release and suggested that he should leave Iran but although he was shaken by this experience he was still patriotically arguing "my country needs me even more".

For another three months all was relatively calm, but once again Iraj was arrested and again incarcerated in Evin. Again after two weeks he was released. Again I spoke to him, but still he insisted that the new regime needed his expertise and he would remain.

Then only one month later he was, for the third time, imprisoned. After his third release, following a most unpleasant two weeks seeing many of his friends and former colleagues executed in the prison compound, he decided that perhaps the new regime did not want him and so, passportless, he walked out over the border into Turkey.

Remembering that Iraj, educated in England and owning a house in Eaton Square, had throughout his working life been in business with British and American companies, it was sickening to me to find that both Britain and the USA had closed its doors to all Iranians. If you were Iranian, you were in the eyes of both governments, an undesirable and thus forbidden to enter. Even the strongest entreaties to MPs, the Foreign Office and even two government ministers were fruitless - Iraj had no passport and was Iranian and that was that.

Fortunately Costa Rica was more tolerant and welcoming and Iraj followed his family there. More than a year later it was the Canadians who offered them sanctuary and passports. Iraj tragically died in 1995, an early death from cancer, almost certainly brought on by the stress of his loss of his country and the apparent abandonment by many of his former friends.

Postscript: in 1990 at a farm management conference I met three Iranian agriculture ministers, all under thirty, all prepared to talk only in the presence of all three of them. They assured me that they knew the Sherkate Sahami Landkesht farm at Torbat-e-Jam and that it was producing far more now than it ever had. Sadly they did not invite me to go and see for myself.

For me the Iranian venture was a great experience and, since the land we farmed was rented, Fountain Farming was able to leave without any financial loss. Indeed for the final four years the operation had made a respectable profit.

SELF EMPLOYED

1980 and new challenges: Andrew, aged 24, working for an American agribusiness company managing vast acreages in Texas, having completed the HND course at Seale-Hayne: Howard, 22, engrossed in Australia in his what is now called a Gap Year, as a jackeroo, having done well at Bristol University: Pip, aged fifteen, rebelling against petty rules at St. Swithuns where she was a weekly boarder.

So there were Hilary and I, living in our vast mansion in Amesbury with twice as much space as we needed, because with the end of Fountain Farming we certainly did not need the accountants' offices, the attached flat or my own huge offices. The tenancy from the Prudential of the 1,350 acre Hedge End Farm in Dorset was mine but it was clear that on its own, especially with its huge bank overdraft, it could not provide either income or employment for an efficient existing farm manager, and me.

Hedge End had once been described to me by John Rowsell, a long-time friend and one of Hampshire's finest farmers, as the second worst farm in Dorset - he never did tell me which he thought was the worst! The problem was that one-third of the farm, 450 very poor acres, had foolishly been cleared of timber in the 1940s and 50s. I offered my landlords, the Pru, the same rent for the better 900 acres as I was paying for the whole 1,350 acres if they would remove these 450 poor acres from the tenancy, which they could then replant with trees. Inexplicably they declined this generous offer.

It was clear therefore that I had to reactivate my consultancy work which had gone into virtual hibernation with Fountain Farming a full time occupation.

I was offered the opportunity to market an electronic immobilising device which had been invented by the Australian

Sheep Association. The device was a simple battery operated appliance which was contained in the body of a large plastic hand-held "torch". One inserted a needle in to the cheek of the animal one wanted to immobilise, a second needle was inserted into the rump, the current switched on and the animal was completely immobilised and anesthetised. It was uncanny to see the effect this had on the animal – and the spectators.

The machine had been developed by the Australian Commonwealth Scientific and Industrial Research Organisation (CSIRO) with the intention of immobilising sheep prior to their being automatically sheared. As far as I know, twenty six years later, they are still trying to automate sheep shearing.

My Australian partner and I formed a company, Feenix International, and took over the worldwide marketing rights of the device – which we called the *Feenix Stockstill* – with the sole restriction that we could not use it in connection with the automatic shearing of sheep.

The *Feenix Stockstill* was a great success with those who saw it demonstrated and we sold more than a thousand in Australia initially. We sent out a questionnaire to users to find out their reactions - all were favourable. One of the questions we posed was "When did you last have a veterinarian on your farm?" One response from an outbacker was "What is a veterinarian?"

This should have been seen as an omen. The main drawback to marketing the *Feenix Stockstill* in other countries was the overt hostility of the vets. At that time vets were, in England, charging about £10, five times the actual cost, for a local anaesthetic on an animal and it would have been difficult for them to justify this fee for using the *Feenix Stockstill*.

The other fear that evoked the antagonism of the vets was their apprehension that our trials were indicating that Rompon (Xylazine), the standard "knock-out" anaesthetic used for complete animal immobility, might well be immobilising the animal but not anaesthetising it, thus allowing the animal to feel pain but not to be able to show any symptoms.

Although I agreed with the British Veterinary Association that we would not market the device in the UK until they had approved its use their antagonism was amazing - a truly extreme case of Ludditeism.

In the USA the vets were more sanguine but the litigation age was upon them and although about 400 ranchers purchased *Feenix Stockstills* their vets were afraid to either use or recommend it.

Having established some useful contacts I travelled to the Argentine in October 1981 and demonstrated it with great success. Together with a local Argentinean vet I took it to a bull breeding centre just outside Buenos Aires. Amongst the bulls there were two prize bulls belonging to General Leopoldo Galtieri, the soon to be defeated President of Argentina, which were about to have some warts surgically removed. I suggested that these would be ideal for the demonstration but, perhaps sensibly bearing in mind the power and position of their owner, the vets suggested we first use the *Feenix Stockstill* on a less august animal. One of the President's Hereford bulls was coaxed into the cattle crush, snorting and infuriated at the indignity of having a bulldog nose-clip inserted into its nostrils to hold its head steady: the vet, carefully removed a number of warts from the animal's dewlap having to stitch two of the more serious cuts he had made: the animal, bleeding profusely, was released from the crush exactly twenty-eight minutes after it had entered.

Now it was our turn and they produced the biggest Friesian bull I have ever seen which needed to be de-horned. The animal was, with difficulty, clamped within the cattle crush, still bucking and bellowing. The electrodes were inserted, one into a cheek and the other near its tailhead, nearly six feet above the ground. When the current was switched on the massive animal went completely rigid and silent as though it had been carved in marble. For some moments there was stunned amazement amongst the spectators, then bedlam as they all crowded around the "statue" to touch and pat it. They could hardly believe this huge animal was totally immobilised.

The vet took the saw and within a minute had removed its two substantial horns: there was virtually no bleeding as the effect of the immobiliser was to tighten the blood vessels. I switched off the current, the bull immediately revived but stood passively in the crush until it was released, when it quietly wandered back into its pen and started to nibble hay. There was loud cheering and much chattering amongst the gauchos, which I took to be favourable, as many of them came forward and shook my hand.

After much discussion and debate it was decided, with great reluctance by some of those present, that they would now operate on the President's second bull using the *Feenix Stockstill*.

The bull was coaxed into the cattle crush and the electrodes inserted and, as with the Friesian bull, there was complete and instant immobility. The vet surgically removed the offending warts with virtually no bleeding: the electrodes were removed: the crush gate opened and, just as the Friesian bull had, the Hereford strolled quietly out. The total exercise had taken two minutes.

The Argentineans were full of enthusiasm and a local dealer wanted the sole marketing rights for the whole of South America which I promised to arrange.

On my return to England in November 1981 I was approached by Ruth Harrison, the author of the 1964 classic book on intensively farmed animals entitled *Animal Machines*. This book was the first to be written on the problems that farmers encountered on intensifying their livestock keeping. At the time of the publication Ruth Harrison became almost a hate figure amongst farmers who considered that how they kept their animals was of no concern to anyone but themselves - a classic case of head-in-sand. The book dealt mainly with veal crates (later banned in the UK but still to be banned elsewhere) and pigs kept on slats as well as battery hens (to be phased out in the UK by 2010). Ruth Harrison played an instrumental role in introducing animal welfare codes to Council of Europe legislation: she died in 2000.

She had heard about the *Feenix Stockstill* and met me at the Farmers' Club to discuss it. Naturally I brought along one of the machines which fascinated her. Much to my surprise and consternation she wanted me to try the device on her. Having used it on myself I was not too worried but for obvious reasons I was not prepared to immobilize her whole body, but duly fitted a pad in place of each of the needles and clipped one to her wrist, the other to the top of her forearm. On switching on the current her lower arm was immobilised and she was quite certain that it was anaesthetised as well. To prove this to herself she took one of the large needles and repeatedly stuck it in to her immobilized arm insisting that she felt nothing.

Following this self-demonstration she became one of the *Feenix Stockstill* strongest supporters, unlike the veterinary profession.

I was working hard on the Argentinean franchise agreement when on Friday 2nd April 1982 I received a letter posted a week earlier from my young interpreter in Buenos Aires, Alexandro Carlos Precedo. He wrote "I hope that it will not affect our friendship or your business but we are taking back (sic) the Malvinas next week".

Later that morning on the 2nd April that the BBC radio reported: *The Argentine Navy with thousands of troops have landed on the Falklands. A small detachment of Royal Marines on the islands put up a brave but futile resistance before Governor Rex Hunt ordered them to lay down their arms. The marine forces were flown to Montevideo along with the British governor.*

Alexandro, along with most of his fellow countrymen, knew that the invasion was going to happen, but apparently the British government didn't. The anti-British fall-out following the Falklands war effectively ended their involvement with the *Feenix Stockstill.*

Unfortunately my Australian partner was an extremely foolish optimist, wrecking a previous otherwise successful project of selling a new grain moisture meter when she had put the company into terminal bankruptcy by massively over-ordering the parts required.

Sadly she had learned nothing from her failure to appreciate the need for a careful control of cash flow. In spite of warnings not to repeat her earlier mistake of over ordering parts, on the strength of a few hundred sales of the *Feenix Stockstil,* she ordered so many *Feenix Stockstill*s that the company ran out of money and CSIRO sensibly took back the marketing rights.

Subsequently the *Feenix Stockstill*s principle was modified for use on humans and became a successful medical tool, especially in dentistry, but the vets have never admitted its efficacy, mainly because it affected them adversely financially. I still receive the odd query for spare parts from outlandish parts of our former empire – the most recent from Timber Creek, a remote habitation in the Australian Northern Territory outback, requesting a replacement *Feenix Stockstill,* twenty five years after buying their first!

The end of yet another era.

CONSULTANCY (1966 onwards)

Consultancy? One is reminded of the castrated tom cat that organised a course of lectures for young toms. The theory was that if you have the know-how but not the equipment set up as a consultant. I started consulting in 1966.

My accountant for the past forty years, John Wilson, was head of the CGA accountancy division and, in 1966 we started Agricultural Management Limited as a wholly owned subsidiary of the CGA with us as joint managing directors. The majority of their clients were landowners or farmers and many required practical advice – this we provided.

A significant number of clients required a mediation service as families so often failed to agree on the most mutually advantageous course of action – this we provided.

All the income which I earned went into the Bury St Austen's Farm account, so that there could be no suggestion that I was earning money at the expense of the farm. Similarly when I became MD of Fountain Farming in 1971 the same applied to my AML earnings. However it was clear in 1972 that the pressures of expanding Fountain Farming meant that I had to give up AML. This I did but I rejoined in 1984.

Outside consultancies too crowded in. For three years, from 1968, I acted as a Strategic Consultant to the Technion in Haifa, which I found fascinating. If only a country not at war (as Israel certainly was) could have instilled such patriotism and morale it would work wonders. I marvelled at the dedication and enthusiasm of the Israelis as they copied, and universally improved, the most modern farming techniques from all over the world. At that time the Israelis had missions in 124 countries. In many fields, especially related to cattle breeding and irrigation, they led the world.

Following the unbundling of Fountain Farming by Stewart Wrightson in 1980 I set up Feenix Farming explaining that Feenix was the old English way of spelling Phoenix: reality was that I wanted to maintain the use of the initials FF since sadly Stewart Wrightson refused to let me take over the name Fountain Farming.

In 1980 I accepted the position of Vice-President of Western Agricultural Management Limited, a farming company based in Fort Collins, Colorado. Western Ag managed huge areas of land in Texas and Nebraska, all based on centre-pivot irrigation. As with Fountain Farming Western Ag purchased land, set it up with the necessary pivots and infrastructure, then sold it to international clients, but, unlike Fountain, Western farmed it as managers for the clients, not as tenants as Fountain did. The actual farming was carried out by self-employed Mennonite farmers who worked with a Western Ag manager. They were brilliant operators and could be relied upon totally.

Each pivot covered 130 acres, leaving 7½ acres unirrigated at each corner of the quarter-section (160 acres) plot. Consistently in the early 1980s Western led the USA championships in yield with many of the pivot areas yielding in excess of six tons of corn (maize) per acre: this was in competition with an average size field of about twenty acres.

Western led the way in accurate assessment of the amount of water required to produce maximum economic yield. The average water usage for Texas in 1983 was 26 inches, Western averaged 17 inches by using accurate underground sensors to determine the crop's water need – rather more accurate than the farmer's boot scraping a dry surface!

Concurrently I was trying to instil some sanity into the manufacture and marketing of the Feenix Stockstill – less successfully. I was farming too, some 3,000 acres in Dorset and Wiltshire, but the two farms were expertly managed by professionals and needed little input (other than capital, mainly borrowed) from me.

In 1984 I was asked by John Wilson to return to Agricultural Management Limited as Joint Managing Director. For three years this was an interesting challenge but by late 1986 the CGA was in crisis and AML ceased to operate.

Having known and admired Sir Emyrs Jones for many years we got together with four other reputable consultants and formed Second Opinion Associates in 1985. The theory was that we would offer our 200 years of combined consultancy experience to large agriculturally oriented organisations to provide them with a second opinion on proposed projects or post-mortems on their failures.

Perhaps we were rather naïve in believing that, for example, the World Bank would want to know what went wrong with the majority of their projects, so many of which failed. Did they really want to know, and hopefully learn from, why they wasted £850 million on building a huge dam between Mauritania, Senegal and Mali? "A cathedral in the desert at which no one wanted to worship" was how it was described by one local guru. Having paid for the dam the World Bank declined to provide funds to teach farmers how to use the water nor would they provide the funds which farmers needed to farm irrigated crops.

By 1988 less than ten per cent of the water in the fast silting up dam was being used. Similarly the construction of the dam completely destroyed the recession agriculture practised further down the rivers. This was a typical failed project of the World Bank but they sadly never learn from their mistakes.

In 1985 I became Chairman of a company which had designed and made a revolutionary digital safe especially for use in hotel bedrooms. It was in this position that I met one of the most charismatic characters of the post-war period, John Stonehouse, founder and then consultant to the company.

John was the last Minister of Aviation before the position was abolished in 1967 he then became Minister of State, Technology. Following a mental breakdown in 1973, he did a "Reggie Perrin", but was arrested in mistake for Lord Lucan (the peer wanted for murder) in Australia on Christmas Eve 1974.

Following his release from prison, he obviously could not resume his previously very successful political career so he wrote half a dozen successful novels and advised a number of technology companies. I was greatly saddened when his heart problems finally got the better of him and he died in 1988, aged 62.

The Mashonaland Development Foundation approached me in 1988 to advise them in Zimbabwe. MDF were a non-political company but did have fourteen members of the Cabinet on the Board. My contact was Sabina Mugabe, sister of the President. It was sickening to see that white farmers in Zimbabwe were completely blind to their inevitable future, should they not change their ways. Blacks were, mainly, treated with contempt by a majority of the 4,200 white farmers who owned eighty per cent of Zimbabwe's farmland.

My first meeting with the largely white Commercial Farmers' Union was a disaster for as soon as they realised that I was working, albeit in an honorary position, for a black organisation I was treated with condescension, polite but aloof. I suggested that the CFU should initiate a black farm managers training scheme and that white farmers should consider giving up about five per cent of their time to devote to black enhancement in every way, but no way was this acceptable.

The atmosphere went decidedly icy when I suggested that if they were not seen to be helping their fellow black countrymen then it was inevitable that they would lose their land. The mere notion was dismissed out of hand, indeed treated with derision. "We keep this country afloat: it is our products that earn the majority of the foreign currency - they could not afford to get rid of us".

President Mugabe was born in Kutama and went to college there, while Sabina Mugabe was the local Member of Parliament. The Jesuit College in 1988 gave the villagers 520 acres of potentially good farmland but with scrub and with trees up to twenty feet high covering the land. The villagers took five months to clear the land by hand but pleas by me to the CFU for a farmer to come in with a tractor to disc the land was treated with contempt. "Why should we help them? They do not appreciate help. They will never learn how to farm". Notice the "theys".

As everyone knows the removal of the white farmers was not going to be hinderered by the certainty that by so doing Mugabe would bankrupt the country, and so it came to pass. Nothing can excuse the behaviour of the massively corrupt Mugabe government but nevertheless one cannot help but wonder if it would have happened in quite this way had the white farmers exhibited a little more sympathy to their fellow men.

In 1988 a young, aged 35, New Zealander Howard Paterson contacted me with the idea of my helping him set up a large scale sheep operation in the UK based on New Zealand principles. After taking him to look at sheep farming in northern England and Scotland, efficiently squired around by my former Fountain Farming Scottish manager, Craig Rankin; I proved conclusively to Howard that it was a non-starter. The relative cost of the resources, both land and livestock, was completely out of kilter with the most optimistic returns.

Howard had made a fortune from property development in New Zealand, especially around his home town of Dunedin and in Hawaii and, although he knew nothing of farming, felt that he wanted to extend his interest into agriculture. Sitting with him at breakfast at the Ritz Hotel in London I suggested that since New Zealand, having recently ended its farm support, was ripe for agricultural expansion he should go in for dairy farming in South Island. Both land and cow prices were at rock bottom in a typical over reaction to the shock of subsidy removal, virtually overnight.

We sketched out the figures on a napkin showing the probable returns from a new 1,000 cow dairy unit.

Howard flew back to Dunedin and I was surprised one year later to receive a phone call from him. Had he gone into dairying? Yes. How many was he milking? 7,200! He had, in less than twelve months, bought the land, the cows, erected the necessary buildings and employed staff, all for £240 a cow place.

He invited me to go and see what they were doing wrong. There was little wrong, except that many of the milking staff were contract milkers while too few were share milkers. There was no doubt that the efficiency of the share milkers far exceeded that of the contract milkers because the share milkers owned the cows, while expenses and returns were shared by the landowner and the share milkers, the interests of the two were effectively identical.

Tasman Agriculture, as the Paterson operation was called, went over to one hundred per cent share milking and within another eighteen months went public with 17,000 cows. By the mid-1990s Tasman were milking 52,000 cows plus a further 10,000 cows in Tasmania.

In addition to advising Tasman I took on the role of Strategic Consultant to many of Howard Paterson's other multifarious enterprises. To name a few - a new egg laying business producing more than one million eggs a day, the largest deer farming operation in the world with more than 100,000 deer, plus numerous pharmaceutical industrial companies which benefited greatly from both his business acumen and financial wizardry. Amongst the numerous pharmaceutical companies in which Howard participated, and in most cases founded, many quickly became leaders in the field of neutraceutical products, including a company producing a biological control of Botrytis in grapes and other susceptible plants.

At that time too Howard was responsible for jointly founding and financing the newly formed A2 Milk Corporation, marketing A2 milk: milk which is being promoted as preventing diabetes, heart disease and many mental illnesses and is free from the potentially damaging beta-casein A1 protein. This was an exciting new concept of milk marketing, which should revolutionise milk production beyond Australasia, with consequent benefits to both consumers and milk producers.

Howard had appointed me their European representative, as European Director of the Otago Trust, Howard's personal investment vehicle, and I was gradually giving up all my other interests to devote my time to this exciting project.

Then on July 1st 2003 tragedy struck: Howard, aged just 50, alone on his balcony overlooking the sea on a business trip to Fiji, failed to awake from a sleep apnoea attack. To add to the woes of the A2 Milk Corporation, the Chief Scientist and Managing Director, died from cancer six weeks later. The company, along with many other Paterson companies, virtually collapsed since it was all too new to have established a reliable sequence of executives. Sadly, even I had to sue the company for outstanding fees. What a tragic end for this unique character: a true lateral thinker to whom New Zealand owes a considerable debt. More than a thousand people attended his funeral in Dunedin, me included.

During the period as I became more involved with Tasman and Howard Paterson I undertook a number of interesting consultancy exercises. In 1992 I worked for the Tata Group in Maharastra, India advising on growing suitable crops for export to the UK. Two years later I did the same for the Maharastra State Marketing Board. It is difficult for Westerners to appreciate that at that time a skilled Indian tractor driver was paid less than fifty pence a day, while a woman farm worker was paid fifteen pence daily. India started to export niche food products in the vegetable and fruit markets.

In 1993 I took part in preparing the five year plan for Algeria contributing the agricultural input to Brown and Roots overall plan, but on the day the final plan was put on the Algerian Prime Minister's desk there was a coup and he was deposed.

Nigeria too accepted some consultancy advice but to little avail. No more successful were my efforts towards solving the Romanian changeover from State to private farming. The indolence of the European Union and the corruption of the Romanians ensured that any help was far too late for useful endeavour. Similarly Estonia benefited not-a-lot from my attempting to convince their Minister of Agriculture that there was no way their dairy farmers could compete with the heavily subsidized butter which Estonia imported from Finland which had recently joined the EU. He, like so many Ministers of agriculture, was not the brightest of businessman. Poland too failed to benefit from Rosen's input. So perhaps I really did need better equipment?

During the 1990s and early 2000s I was encouraging British farmers to buy land in either New Zealand or Tasmania. As Howard Paterson realized at that time the New Zealand land prices were so low that one could actually show a ten per cent return on total capital involved. But by the end of the century land prices had rocketed and this particular attraction ended.

However land in Tasmania is still today absurdly cheap and a farmer can still earn at least ten per cent on the total capital invested. Contrary to popular myth Tasmania is an attractive island of sixteen million acres with a most clement climate and friendly people.

Sadly I found, together with my New Zealand and Tasmanian partners, that the average British expatriate farmer could not be trusted to meet his obligations. We arranged for a considerable number of British farmers to visit both countries but it was impossible to do other than trust the would-be immigrant to pay the fees we charged. For example it was agreed that if a farmer purchased a farm while we were showing them the country they would pay us the 1½ per cent finder's fee. A number of people simply did not buy while we were showing them suitable properties but returned on a later visit and purchased property, thus avoiding the fee. Frankly we, especially my overseas partners, were horrified at the low moral standards of many of the farmers whom we introduced to these countries. They were not a good advertisement for Britain.

There were, of course, exceptions, farmers who happily paid our finder's fee and have gone on to enjoy the respect of the locals in the countries in which they now live and farm.

THE FARMERS' CLUB

One of the most satisfying, and certainly the most prestigious, of extra mural activities which I undertook was with the Farmers' Club. Founded by a farsighted group of farmers in 1842 the Club has thrived at its present location in Whitehall Court since 1904.

When I became a member in 1967, after using the Club's facilities for some time while engaged in other activities, such as the FBA and FMA, there were 5,196 members with the distinguished farmer and soldier, Colonel Jack Houghton Brown, DSO. TD, as Chairman.

One of the great strengths of the Club is its insistence that two-thirds of the members are practising farmers, while the remaining one-third have to be closely allied to agriculture. This assures that politicians, bankers, consultants, media and even land agents can claim to be agricultural involved.

Two year later I was invited to join the committee, chaired by the brave (subsequently to drown trying to rescue a yachtsman in distress) Jack Merricks BEM and it was at a time when the Club was faced with a severe financial crisis. The new owners of Whitehall Court told all the leaseholders in the huge building that they either had to agree to a new ninety nine year lease or depart. The sum demanded for the club premises was £140,000, a formidable sum for its members to raise. Many of the existing clubs with premises in Whitehall Court simply disappeared.

A letter was despatched to all Farmers' Club members, but by return of post came a cheque for the full amount from the great poultry man the late Jack (later Sir John) Eastwood. Thus the Club was able to embark on a continuous improvement in its facilities which still continues today.

In 1975, as Chairman of the House Committee, I instigated two rules which I am delighted to say are still enforced today. There was to be no smoking in the dining room and only British cheeses would be served there.

Fortuitously when I became Chairman of the Club in 1978, following in the impressive footsteps of Somerset farmer, Roland Stewart Sandeman, more property in Whitehall Court became available, alongside our existing property. We needed £45,000 to purchase this: once more Jack came to the rescue and wrote out the necessary cheque. He also asked how much it would require to improve the kitchens and move the bar and Club offices: again he handed over a cheque for the necessary £45,000. Also at that time it was decided to rebuild the virtual prefab pavilion which the Club owned on the Royal Showground. This time Jack agreed to meet half the estimated cost of £45,000, a benefactor indeed.

However, following our presentation to him (accompanied by his PA, later to become Sir David Naish, President of the NFU), of a beautifully carved wooded plaque to commemorate his generosity and the opening of the new pavilion at the 1978 Royal Show, he asked how much the renovation actually cost. Reluctantly I confessed that it had cost £54,000. Without hesitation Jack then and there wrote out at cheque for the whole £54,000.

Later Jack continued to finance a great many improvement schemes at the Club. No one should wonder why the Club proudly boasts an Eastwood Room with his portrait reigning benignly over the fireplace – a generous and kindly man.

The Club at that time organised about four London-based important agricultural seminars every year. One of the traditions that had been formalised over many years was that any incoming Minister of Agriculture made his first public statement to the Club members. It was only in 1997 that this sensible tradition ceased with the election of the virulently anti-farmer, and agriculturally ignorant, Labour government.

The first meeting which I had to chair was when Agriculture Minister John Silkin asked the Club to provide a forum, for the second time, for his résumé of his first four hundred days in office. The meeting was somewhat fraught since the old maxim that farmers vote Conservative but pray for a Labour government was being massively disproved at that time.

In April 1975 the government had issued a White Paper *Food from Our Own Resources*, twenty pages of political claptrap, which supposedly had the aim of, to put it bluntly, Britain producing unlimited quantities of food. As the White Paper stated: *The Government takes the view that a continuing expansion of food production in Britain will be in the national interest.*

Unfortunately in true political style the words were far greater than the deed. Thus I gave my copy of the White Paper to Pip, our then ten year old daughter, who proceeded to draw in coloured pictures to illustrate it.

At the meeting with John Silkin the suitably illustrated document was on the table between us. He asked why it was illustrated, to which I responded that if one was going to read a fairy story one should at least have pretty pictures. This was to set the mood for the meeting.

More than four hundred Farmers' Club members, mainly irate farmers, gave the Minister a hard time, but consummate politician that he was, Silkin was unfazed. Just as I was about to close the meeting a distinguished farmer, and labour supporter, decided to quote Cromwell's statement to the Long Parliament when he thought it was no longer fit to conduct the affairs of the nation: *"You have sat too long here for any good you have been doing. Depart, I say, and let us have done with you. In the name of God, go."*

Before I could interject the member went on to ask the assembled members to pass a vote of no confidence in the Minister and to suggest that the Minister should be asked to resign from the Club.

Quite a baptism of fire for my first Club meeting as Chairman. Hurriedly I suggested that the Minister was very aware of how farmers were feeling and that any such motion from the floor was out of order. Although Silkin did not resign he never set foot in the Club again.

Even in those far off days one of the major perks of being Chairman was to invite the two main guests for the Club's Annual Dinner, for 1,200 members, including spouses, at the Grosvenor House Hotel in December during the Smithfield Show week. My two guests were His Excellency Kingman Brewster, US Ambassador to the Court of St James and the financier Jimmy (later Sir James) Goldsmith. Both performed brilliantly and I basked in the reflected glory.

Goldsmith was then famous (or should that be notorious?) for his public statement that "Marrying your mistress creates a vacancy". When I went to Goldsmith's office in September (1978) to tie up any loose ends, I asked him who would be accompanying him to the dinner? "Annabel of course", was his response; I asked what name we should use for her since at that time he was not married to her. What is the date of the dinner, he enquired? When I told him that it was the 8th December, he immediately responded that he would marry Annabel on the 2nd - to make it simpler for the programme!

One drama during my year of office was a deficiency in the Club's restaurant accounts. Although we were making a respectable profit in both the bar and the letting of the bedrooms, the restaurant had continually lost money. We instructed our accountants, who had been with the Club since it was founded in 1842, to carry out an audit. This they did and assured us that the loss we were making on meals was normal and no malpractice was involved. Their conclusion was supported by an outside firm of caterers who insisted that no Clubs made a profit on their restaurants.

By a strange set of fortuitous coincidences it transpired that our house manageress, who always had her sister stand in for her when away (which should perhaps have made us suspicious) had been cleverly milking the Club of about £15,000 a year by issuing her own forged invoices to any member paying cash. Holloway housed her for a year and our, now former, accountants repaid all the money that the Club had lost.

Today the Farmers' Club, with its fifty-two comfortable bedrooms, committee rooms and superb restaurant, is prospering mightily with 5,568 members, among which are many keen young Under-30s, happily paying the lowest subscription of any London club. For the past few years the Chairman of the Club, appointed annually, is occupied virtually full time publicising the Club around the country, with great success.

JOURNALISM (1982 onwards)

Although I had had the occasional article published in the farming press (my first in 1968 in the now long extinct *Farmer & Stockbreeder*) it came as a total surprise to receive an invitation in 1982 from Marcus Oliver to write a weekly column in the soon to be published weekly *Farming News*. I really could not imagine how I could put 1,040 interesting words on paper on a weekly basis, especially when Marcus suggested that the *Farming News* anticipated circulating more than 100,000 copies a week.

I tried to compromise with the proposal of a monthly column but Marcus, one of the best agricultural editors of the past forty years (in spite of being a devout vegetarian), insisted it had to be a weekly column, but it would be well rewarded at £275 a time. I agreed, on the understanding that it would be for a trial period of three months and Marcus would regularly feed me ideas to write about.

In 2001, when *Farming News* ceased publication, some nineteen years later, foolishly terminated by a publisher who seemed to be unaware of the considerable influence of the paper, especially amongst politicians, I was still regularly writing for it and Marcus, and his two successors, had only once chosen to provide a suggestion for a subject. After its demise there was a great outcry, especially from members of the House of Lords, that the paper would be much missed for providing a non-establishment line on agricultural politics.

A weekly column in *Farming News* really was a superb platform in which to express my views but, after a few years of constantly needling the readers, especially on the stupidity of farm subsidies and the corruption in Europe, it became clear that one was either preaching to the converted – or the unconvertible.

There was never a week when there was not a hot topic on which I was anxious to express my views and the words flowed. Until

146

my computer arrived around 1996, I handwrote every word, this to be sub-edited and then finally typed by my long-suffering wife.

Marcus made it clear that my job was to create discussion and I do believe that my column met this objective judging by readers' responses: some virulently anti, some neutral and a minority in agreement. With the corrupt European Union, allied to the so-called Common Agricultural Policy, dominating the public arena, there was a continual flow of subjects for me, many based on the EU politicians' misdeeds. If any public company directors were as provenly corrupt as the EU politicians they would be languishing in jail.

As a long time believer that farm subsidies are a pernicious influence on farmers' activities, I suggested that the subsidy aided farmer was no different from the drug addict awaiting his next fix, their brains permanently damaged. Somehow this was not a widely accepted view amongst farmers during the 1980s and 1990s, although occasionally sense would prevail and farmers gradually, oh so very gradually, came to accept that farm subsidies ensured that they remained second-class citizens awaiting their public handouts.

The prominent large-scale Cambridgeshire farmer, Oliver Walston, became even more unpopular than me with the subsidy-addicts, when he proudly publicised his annual subsidy cheque, usually around £200,000, in the press and on television and said "thank you very much".

An advantage to being a member of the Guild of Agricultural Journalists was the access this provided to those in the "corridors of power". Three weeks after the indecent imposition of milk quotas on dairy farmers I confronted the Minister of Agriculture, Michael Jopling, about the absurd acceptance by the British government of both the concept of quotas themselves and the absurdly low allocation of quota to Britain. The Irish government secured nearly six times as much quota per head of the population as did Britain: even the Dutch secured three times as much per head.

Milk quotas were a disastrous imposition from which the British dairy industry has yet to recover more than twenty years later. The Minister however insisted to me that all British dairy farmers could stand "a nine per cent cut in profits". When I protested that a nine per cut in output did not correlate with a nine per cent cut in profits, Jopling insisted that it did. He never understood that it was the last pig in the litter that produced the profit – to muddle my metaphors. A nine per cut in milk output, in my calculations, represents a cut in profits of at least forty per cent because none of the farmers' other costs could realistically be reduced, at least not in the short-term.

In 1986 I was approached by the right-wing Centre for Policy Studies to produce a paper on the future of farming for publication by them. When I submitted an eighteen page document laid out in similar style to a government White Paper, entitled *Farming and the Nation,* they appeared happy. However a week later it became clear that the then Minister of Agriculture, Michael Jopling, was not happy that an outsider should tarnish the White Paper concept and that if the government felt a White Paper was required, he would write it. CPS politely told me to take my paper elsewhere. *Farming News* published it and sold 5,000 copies at £2.00 each, complete with my new crest and logo *Ne Quid Nimis* ("Let nothing be in excess"). Twenty years later, even with hindsight, I would not alter a word.

Early in 1988 I was approached by the internationally renowned Professor Jimmye Hillman, of the University of Arizona, to front a film which they were intending to make about world agriculture. After considerable discussions the producer, Larry Klaas, and I settled on the title *"Feast amid Famine - the paradox of plenty."*

On Sunday 11 September 1988 three Americans, complete with 250 pounds of filming equipment, landed on our doorstep: Larry

Klaas who was the producer with his wife Deborah as sound recordist and Glenn the cameraman. No time was lost in filming around Britain before we set off on our hectic programme overseas. On Wednesday 14 September we flew, via Lisbon, to the Cape Verde Islands where we seemed to cover most of its one million acres for the film.

Then on Saturday, thanks to the rather unreliable Cape Verde Airlines, we landed behind schedule at Dakar Airport in Senegal, only to see our onward Air Mauritania fight taxiing out from dispersal. We prevailed on our pilot to stop beside the 727 jet and ask the Air Mauritania jet to wait for us – to our amazement, it did. The four of us climbed down, hi-jacked a passing airport trolley and loaded our filming equipment into the hold of the 727. Then, ignoring the minor problem of checking in, we climbed aboard, ticketless.

Had we known that Mauritania is justifiably considered to be the "pit of the world" perhaps we would not have been so keen to arrive in the capital city of Nouachott. Every city has its slums but this city simply was a slum with but two "oases", the Saudi donated mosque and a new Novotel hotel.

What can one say about Mauritania that is not derogatory? In my opinion if there is one country which will be uninhabitable by man within fifty years it will be Mauritania. In our travels we saw no future for the three million inhabitants of this poor benighted land.

To our amazement there was a plague of locusts there too – what on earth were they eating? The Canadian pilots of the spraying aircraft, brought in to control the locusts, were bemoaning the banning of DDT for there is no efficient alternative chemical for killing the locusts. But, because it was the (very limited) rainy season there was some spectacular scenery to be filmed. But where there had been forests only a quarter of a century earlier there was now desert. As I write this (September 2006), thirty years after DDT was banned in most countries, the World Health Organisation has announced that DDT should be used again – where necessary. A most wise decision.

Taking off to Casablanca on an Air Morocco flight it was the first time that I had heard a cabin full of passengers actually clapping on leaving a country: what a depressing nation.

Filming in Morocco was a wonderful surprise, full of colour and exciting agriculture: then on to France to film the other side of the paradox. The results of massive support for sugar production exemplified the whole raison d'etre for the film. And so on to filming in Thailand, Australia and New Zealand. We also filmed an interview with the brilliant American academic Clayton Yeutter, US Secretary for Agriculture at the time: together with Enoch Powell one of the greatest intellects it has been my privilege to meet. The film won the USA Gold Award for an Agricultural Educational film in 1989.

Later further filming and writing were undertaken and a second film, *"The Miracle of Agriculture"* was completed; this won both the 1990 Gold Award and the Award for the Best Educational Aid in the USA. Larry Klaas went on to produce more than 300 very successful agriculturally based films, before dropping out to skipper a sailboat in Mississippi.

The British Food and Farming Year celebrations in 1988 included the 150 page book, *England's Pleasant Land – vision and reality*: a coffee table book which sold 9,000 copies, my views on the reality of English farming, the vision replicated with breathtaking pictures by the celebrated artist and our friend David Mynett.

The Lord Plumb of Coleshill, ex-President of the NFU and then President of the European Parliament, flattered us both by writing: "This is not only a very beautiful book it is also vital reading for anyone who wants to understand what is really happening on our land today. At last the English farmer has a book to be proud of."

150

Then in 1991 came my second White Paper, again published by *Farming News*, written in sheer desperation and complete despair of the Conservative government ever understanding what British farming needed – here I clearly differentiate between "farming" and "farmers": what is best for the former is not necessarily best for the latter, and vice-versa.

Entitled *"The Reform of the Common Agricultural Policy"* my intention was to put together sufficient evidence to achieve its major objective, which was: "The writer believes that the only way forward lies in the removal, over a strictly limited period, of all trade-distorting and food-production subsidies."

At that time the CAP was costing the twelve nations of the European Community in excess of £260 million per day.

Then, as now, I have no doubts at all that the majority of British farmers would be far better off if Britain left the EU and followed New Zealand's example of ending farm subsidies. This would allow farmers to make decisions based on their true resources rather than simply awaiting their annual fix. So, in 1991, I managed to convince enough sponsors, about fifteen in all (nine from Britain), to allow nine carefully selected young (-ish) agriculturists to spend a month in New Zealand with the challenge to answer the question "Is there a life after subsidies?"

The nine, all under forty years of age, comprised practical farmers and agricultural consultants. The New Zealanders, particularly Ann Taylor of the NZ Dairy Board, were mightily helpful, both practically and financially. Their Federated Farmers, Dairy Board, Apples and Pears Board, and Meat Board all helped and also ferried the ten of us all over the two islands, proving the correctness of the New Zealand farmers' decision to go to their government in 1985 calling for the ending of farm subsidies.

Out of the 30,000 NZ farmers only 800 went out of business, and even these were given enough money to buy a house. It was impossible to find a NZ farmer who wished to return to charity handouts, otherwise known as subsidies. As one proud NZ farmer responded when I asked if he regretted the ending of government support, "Anthony, it is impossible to stand tall with your hand out".

I was delighted, and proud, when our nine participants produced the final document coming down unanimously with the answer "yes". Should I therefore have been surprised when one participant, an NFU county chairman who surmised on his return that "It would be beneficial for the industry to be market-led and not misdirected by bungling politicians", backed down when faced with a public challenge at the following NFU AGM?

In 1990 I was approached by the BBC Radio farming department to host a series of "Breakfast with ...." programmes which are still running successfully after so many years. The first "victim" was my long time friend, Professor John Nix of Wye College who has done so much for spreading the gospel of practical farm economics. My further interviewees included Brian Chamberlin, the New Zealander who did so much for his country as President of Federated Farmers, Trade Envoy to the Uruguay GATT Round and as agricultural attaché in London. I also convinced the BBC that I should travel to the USA and internationalise the programme by breakfasting with John Harris, an exceptional California farmer and US Secretary of State Clayton Yeutter, who had already taken part in our films. With his strictly limited time the programme was totally unedited and he was superb. Another success was the perfect English speaker Professor Jaroslav Voracek from Prague.

But undoubtedly the outstanding success of the series of breakfasts was when Dr Tony O'Reilly filled in almost the entire twenty-five minutes with a succession of Irish stories as well as emphasising his pithy views on the absurdity of the CAP. This programme received such critical acclaim that it was repeated twice.

I became sadly disabused with the BBC Farming Programme when, it having been agreed that I should approach Prime Minister John Major and US Ambassador to London Ray Seitz to take part, the BBC decided that neither was sufficiently agriculturally oriented to be worth recording. An amazingly insulting decision about the UK Prime Minister and the Ambassador for our greatest agricultural competitor.

Later in 1991 I performed at the Irish Guild of Agricultural Journalists in Dublin, sharing the platform with the Irish hero, European Commissioner Macsharry, the man responsible for ensuring that Irish farmers claimed the most per head of all European farmers. It was not a pretty sight but I think the audience enjoyed the blood.

My influence on farming? Farmers today require youthful enthusiasm to survive the carping of the ignorant, including many within their own industry, and must learn that all the while they are seen to be so heavily in hock to government funds they will never regain the respect of others. Farming will not thrive until farmers throw off the yoke of government control which will only be achieved once the older brain-damaged-by-subsidies farmers hand over to the younger generation. Perhaps it is rather extreme to suggest that farmers should be offered the choice at age fifty-five – retirement or compulsory euthanasia?

Although my business dealings with non-farming New Zealanders have caused me great regret and scorn for many of them, I still respect their farmers who, twenty years ago, took the dramatic step of refusing government support and thus have been able to stand tall, brains undamaged by subsidies, their own masters.

Whilst in many walks of life individualism is to be admired and respected, it is this trait in British farmers which has hampered collaborative ventures: certainly successive governments have used this eccentricty as an effective weapon against farmers.

Whereas farmers express the view that "a sheep's worst enemy is another sheep", in reality one could well believe, from the almost complete lack of co-operation between farmers, that "a farmer's worst enemy is another farmer". Sadly many years of government subsidies have led to a greed amongst too many older farmers who have come to expect respect whilst doing little to earn it.

Today British agriculture is in even bigger chaos than in the darkest days of the 1920s and 1930s. The main difference today is that the fashionable requirement for a wealthy man to own land, combined with absurdly generous inheritance tax avoidance of agricultural land, has resulted in astronomical farmland prices. Prices of up to £10,000 an acre for trendy Hampshire farms are not uncommon. One can only smile wryly at turning down Sussex farms fifty years ago because they fetched sixty pounds an acre. Or even Fountain Farming's first purchase in Hampshire thirty-five years ago at £312 an acre.

I will be forever grateful that at least I farmed for thirty of the forty modern golden years of British agriculture – 1956 to 1986, missing the earlier ten golden years before 1956. This era of farming prosperity was second only to the original fifty golden years from 1812 to 1862. How many people know that the actual ex-farm price of wheat in 1812 was £28 a ton: a figure not equalled until 1973?

Farmers were the envy of the populace but were respected too. Farming, in my day, was not only a worthwhile challenge but was also fun.

Perhaps my most enjoyable public performance was to the First Palermo Agribusiness Conference in Buenos Aires in July 2002, before an audience of five hundred. My brief was to explain the subsidies and tariffs which many countries imposed to support domestic food production - an easy task for I knew of no subsidies which could even remotely be justified. Although it was an international audience, the majority was South American, where there are effectively no agricultural subsidies, indeed many South American governments tax their farmers' foreign exports.

At that time the USA was promoting a massive increase in farm support which they were proposing in their new 2002 Farm Bill. Fellow speaker Mrs.Carol Brookins, the American Director of the World Bank, was truly facing a dilemma. She had for many years expressed outright hostility to all farm support but following her recent appointment to the diplomatic post of World Bank director she had to toe her government's line and defend the indefensible.

I have never attended a better organized conference: there was simultaneous translation (Spanish and English) and every modern electronic aid available, all efficiently operating. My power-point presentation was in both Spanish and English and the slides appeared exactly on cue.

Because the presentations by Carol Brookins and me were so diametrically opposing, the conference organizers arranged an extra debate on the subject of subsidies between the two of us. Needless to say I won easily as there were few in the audience who supported the selfish American line. It was obvious to all that the new US Farm Bill was aimed directly at domestic voters in the forthcoming elections.

Subsequently I have written many agricultural obituaries for which I have found my personal contacts within agriculture invaluable.

When my very old friend and mentor, Sir Emrys Jones died in 2000, another mutual friend suggested to the *Times* that I should write his obituary. I was honoured, for Emrys as Director General of ADAS, served agricultural ministers as diverse as Fred Peart and Christopher Soames and yet never once let down those who he really considered to be the ones who mattered, the farmers and the consumers.

In 1973 Emrys, partly in growing frustration at the thought of European interference in both British politics and British farming, resigned from the civil service with the intention of becoming chairman of Fountain Farming.

Unhappily for Fountain, but to the considerable benefit of the Royal Agricultural College at Cirencester, his resignation took effect at the time of the Poulson Affair. Politicians had decided that civil servants should not work with companies within their own sphere of influence until two years had passed after leaving office, except with their minister's special permission. For reasons still unknown this permission was refused in Emrys' case.

So, whilst Fountain was denied the valuable benefit of Emrys' thirty three years of impressive agricultural experience, the RAC at Cirencester offered Emrys the position of Principal. He accepted this onerous role and set about revolutionising the running of the College, especially concentrating on raising the considerable funds necessary to ensure the College's continuing prosperity. It was, again, an imposing accomplishment as Emrys set the College on the road to eminence in the field of agricultural education. In 1978, after completing his promised five year stint as principal, Emrys retired to the Wolds of Lincolnshire to enjoy further his favourite pastime of game shooting at which he excelled. Emrys was a friend, a close friend, and the eulogy flowed so easily.

Today the only outlet for my journalistic skills lies in a fairly regular requirement for these agricultural obituaries in the *Times* and the occasional article. Ironically, as a professional journalist for twenty-six years and, having written a regular column in *Farming News* for twenty years, together with numerous other articles, I never had a column censored and certainly never one spiked – until last year……….

In the appendix I have reprinted an article I wrote for the British Nuffield Scholars Newsletter since I felt so strongly about the dangerous path the white South African farmers appeared to be taking. Staggeringly the Nuffield Director spiked the article on the basis that it was too contentious for Zimbabwean Nuffield scholars. It has since appeared in other places, including the *Times*.

TRAVELLING (1984 - 2006)

Little did I realise when I asked S.F.Martin to organise a tour for the Farm Buildings Association in 1964 that this would sow the seed for me to organise overseas tours for farmers: Martin went on to found the still successful Agricultural Travel Bureau. The purpose of the original meeting was to set up a two week tour for FBA members to visit Holland and Switzerland. The basic arrangements became rather more complicated when nearly fifty of the eighty four travellers declined to fly, preferring to travel by train.

The rail travellers set off on Sunday 2nd May 1965, while the intrepid flyers followed a day later, all meeting up in Amsterdam at noon. We roamed far and wide across Holland, admiring their very sophisticated farm buildings: they were great exponents of laminated timber use. An emotional visit was made too to the Arnhem Airborne Forces War Cemetery, 21 years after the disastrous Bridge-Too-Far raid.

On Friday evening the group divided again, to move on to Zurich, the train travellers spending the night in the train. Then we all spent a fascinating week looking at wildly uneconomic, but luxurious, farming across Switzerland, hosted by the late Hans Hauser, the owner of Bucher-Guyer agricultural machinery who later became a good friend. Swiss farmers were paid for their crops according to their height above sea level, then as now.

We marvelled at the unlimited spending, being especially impressed by one new circular concrete dairy building: the fodder was on the top floor, the cows one floor down, then on the ground floor the manure storage.

Swiss hospitality was most enjoyable and one thing I learned then, and later, was that farmers spoke with a common voice, irrespective of whether it was based on German, French, Spanish or English.

But the setting up and running of Fountain Farming precluded any more organising of farmers' tours until my next venture in 1984 when I took a most exclusive group of arable farmers to Illinois, USA.

We travelled in a mini-coach, the luxury of which I have never since experienced. Everyone had their own armchair, there was TV and video, a microwave oven and everything one could possibly want, including the kitchen sink.

Just prior to departing for Chicago on Monday 28th May I had tried, with my journalist's hat firmly in place, to fix up a meeting with the United States Secretary for State for Agriculture, John Block, who lived near our route. Unfortunately it was a bad time for Block because one of his farming business partners was being arraigned on fraud charges and thus there was a strict "no interviews with journalists" response.

As we drove past the end of the road which led to the Block farms I told our driver the story of the refused interview. Later that evening the driver proudly announced that if I wanted to meet Secretary Block he would be available at 08.30 am the next morning, a Saturday. Thus it was that a group of interested British farmers had a fascinating private meeting and farm tour with the US Secretary of Agriculture, arranged by our coach driver, something our Foreign Office had failed to achieve. We gained an interesting insight too into American politics: John Block had never been elected to any official position – he was simply asked by President Reagan to fill this controversial post.

In spite of the success of this tour it was not until 1987 that my serious travelling business became a significant part of my activities (see Appendix).

In June 1987 I took a group of twenty five farmers, mainly together with their wives, to Texas and Oklahoma. We were feted throughout the tour with massive local press coverage because we were, in most places, the first foreign farmers the locals had ever seen.

It was so successful that we repeated the tour in November. But this time there were forty-two travellers, which I then realised was far too many for comfort. With one exception I fixed a maximum of travellers in future to twenty as being the ideal number from every point of view.

The demand amongst farmers and their wives was to see how their counterparts lived in other countries and I quickly built up a number of loyal followers who travelled with me at least once a year.

Gradually over the next twenty years, as I and my supporters aged, the tours became more and more rural holidays taken in a leisurely fashion. I set the target of the ideal day as: departure, after a leisurely breakfast, at 9.00am, one agricultural visit (avoiding research stations and college farms, as being too serious) and one 'tourist' visit, returning to the same hotel by 5.00pm. As a generalisation this proved to be a popular formula and close to a thousand travellers have confirmed this.

The one question which I find it different to answer is "which is your favourite country?" It is impossible to choose between the amazing, often awe inspiring, countries on my travel list. Where do you place the amazing "discovery" of Welsh speakers, ten thousand of them, who settled in Argentinean Patagonia in 1856 but, so I was assured by the three Welsh speakers travelling with me, still speaking identical Welsh today?

Then coming upon intensive vegetable production in Tasmania where the superb grade one topsoil was more than thirty feet deep? One of my travellers taking over the bullock-drawn plough preparing the ground for potatoes some 10,000 feet high in the Andes? And so on? And so on.......

However I do believe that there are five places on this earth that should figure on every traveller's list.

160

For wild game viewing there cannot, in my experience, be anywhere more impressive than the Masai Mara in Kenya. To go there and see the wild animals in their natural habitat is an honour and a privilege. And no, in my experience, neither the Okavango Delta nor any of the game parks in South Africa can compete, especially with the sheer magnitude of the Mara. Sadly today one has to beware of the bandits.

For impressive scenery it would be difficult to find anything to compete with the Iguazu Falls, between Brazil and Argentine. Strung out along the rim of a crescent-shaped cliff some 2½ miles long, comprising 275 individual cascades and waterfalls plummetting up to 269 feet into the gorge below. The thunderous roaring can be heard from miles away. These outstanding falls make Niagara look like a leaking bucket.

But of course these falls must rank in inspiring splendour alongside the Torres del Paine (Cuernos del Paine) in the Paine National Park in Patagonia: where else can one watch, happily photographing for hours, while the sunrise dramatically changes the colours of these massive titons? There are millions of acres of dramatic land and mountains, some 1700 miles south of Santiago, which make up the semi-arid desert of Patagonia, in both Chile and Argentina.

Then there is the Great Barrier Reef, off the Queensland coast of Australia, surely one of the natural wonders of the world? There are about 2,800 coral reefs stretching over 1,500 miles. The locals boast that it is the largest structure on the planet built by living organisms, its coral rampart hosts a carnival of sea life, a peerless place to snorkel or dive.

But for sheer uniqueness there can be nowhere in the world which can compare with the Galapagos Islands, straddling the equator some 600 miles off the coast of Ecuador. The correct name for these twenty one significant islands is the Archipiélago de Colón, comprising nearly 2 million acres of land with fewer than 12,000 people living there.

Charles Darwin, in the Beagle, visited the Galapagos Islands in 1835, where he studied and noted the similarities and differences of the flora and fauna. He concluded that the species, to survive, would gradually alter based on environmental conditions.

After more than twenty years of his life gathering supporting evidence, Darwin published *"The Origin of the Species by Natural Selection"* in 1859.

It took another 119 years before the Islands were declared a World Heritage site by UNESCO in 1978, underlining their universal value for mankind. Do not be put off by supposed ruination of the islands by tourism.

About three million people tourists visit the 93,000 acre Isle of Wight, which is populated by 135,000 inhabitants. The Galapagos Islands are more than twenty times as big and receive fewer that 60,000 tourists annually and no one is allowed ashore unless accompanied by an approved naturalist guide. Private yacht owners are heavily fined if they abuse the local regulations and anchor in the islands, except at Puerto Ayora on Santa Cruz Island.

After seven visits, together with more than hundred fellow travelers, I would happily return tomorrow to this matchless place.

I will be eternally grateful to all those faithful followers who have, by their own enthusiasm, enabled me to show them so much of the world. Including my consultancy visits I have visited more than a hundred countries – so far!

IN CONCLUSION

So, many words later, I come to the end of these mainly pleasant memories and thankfully send this tome to the printers, giving thanks for seventy five interesting years. I have been blessed with a remarkable wife, always supportive and devoted to us all, three exceptional children and numerous grandchildren who give us the greatest pleasure. Indeed soon after the memoirs are printed we expect to be great-grandparents to Melanie's and Dustin's first child.

Healthwise the family has been relatively fortunate, it is only in very recent years that the toll of old age is beginning to limit Hilary's and my activities, me more so.

Andrew, who gave up an influential position in large scale global agriculture to become a paramedic fireman, is as happy as the days are long carrying out his challenging and worthwhile role in Fort Collins, Colorado. One can only wish that his opposite numbers in Britain were treated with the same respect and admiration as they are in the USA – they are heroes.

Locally to him, Shelby (married in 2005 to Kara) is building up a very successful heating business in Steamboat Springs, while Melanie (engaged to Dustin, a heating engineer in Loveland, Colorado) is busy preparing for the birth of Evan Thomas around December 4th.

Not far from us in Hampshire, Howard and Sue are the justifiably proud parents of Lucy (14), Ella (11) and Lydia (7), their three bright and beautiful daughters. Howard, having spent fourteen years building up Compaq computers in the UK, lives in a lovely house only thirty-five minutes away and is now actively engaged in property development in Bulgaria.

Also in Hampshire, Pip, running a Veterinary Locum agency, and Pete, an all-too-rare master craftsman, are in the process of moving house when they will once again dramatically improve yet another property.

It is now more than fifty-two years since I entered the unique field of agriculture and I give thanks that I farmed when it really was fun. Farmers were respected then and contributed to the health and wealth of Britain in every way.

Life has been kind and certainly never dull…………..

CURRICULUM VITAE

Address: Six Chattis Hill, Spitfire Lane, Stockbridge, Hampshire
SO20 6JS UK

Tel: 01264-810135 Email: antrosen@ aol.com

Born: 19th December 1930, British

Status: Married, Hilary, 5th August 1954: three adult offspring

Andrew 6th Feb 1956: Howard 25th Jan 1958: Pip 18th
Mar 1965

Education: 1940-48 Framlingham College, Suffolk

Brighton Technical College

Royal Artillery, Captain (Air OP Pilot)

East Sussex School of Agriculture

Advanced Farm Business Management Course, Wye

1974 Henley Business School Management Course

Past positions:

1956-64   Farms Manager, 640 acres West Sussex

Managing tenant partner, 1700 acres, West Sussex

Founder MD Agricultural Management Limited

1968-71   Strategic Consultant, Technion, Haifa, Israel

Founder MD, Fountain Farming Limited, 30,000 ac

Founder MD, Sherkate Sahami Landkesht, Iran 6,500 ac

Strategic Consultant, Agricultural Management Ltd

Consultant, Feenix International Pty, Australia

1980-90   Vice-President, Western Agricultural Management, USA

Tenant/partner, 3,000 acres (ex-FF)

165

	Managing partner, 360 acres
	Director, Agricultural Management Limited
1985-90	Partner, Second Opinion Associates
	Chairman, Earnison Holdings plc
	Consultant, Mashonaland Foundation, Zimbabwe
	Consultant, Tasman Agriculture Limited, New Zealand
	Consultant, Tata Exports, India
1993	Consultant, Strategic Agricultural Plan for Algeria
1993	Consultant, Strategic Agricultural Plan for Nigeria
1994	Consultant, Maharastra State Marketing Board, India
1993-95	Consultant, Romanian Agricultural Privatisation Project
1995	Consultant, Estonia
	Consultant, Poland
1983-2001	Political and Economic Columnist, Farming News
1988-2003	Strategic Agribusiness Consultant to Howard Paterson NZ
2000-2003	Strategic Consultant, A2 Milk Corporation NZ
2001-2003	European Director, The Otago Trust NZ

Present: 1980-Chief executive (and owner) Feenix Farming, International Agribusiness Consultant

Positions: 1984-Anthony Rosen Travel (sole owner since 1997)

Hobbies: Work, photography and travel (visited 106 countries)

Extra mural:

1958-	Life member of Royal Association of Dairy Farmers
	Farm Buildings Association (Chairman 1965)

Life member of Farmers' Club (Chairman 1978)

Founder member of Farm Management Association

1971   Founder: the International Farm Management Association

Oxford Farming Conference Committee

1967   Nuffield Scholar

Founder: The '75 Club (Chairman '71, '84 & '90)

Awarded Winston Churchill Fellowship

BBC Agricultural Advisory Committee

Agricultural Forum

1984-   Member, Guild of Agricultural Journalists

1985-   Member, International Federation of Ag Journalists

Organiser World Food Summit, Brussels

Founder Director, Green Eagle Golf

Publications:

1959-   Frequent articles as freelance journalist

1982-2001   Political and Economic Columnist, Farming News

1986   "Farming and the Nation" – White Paper

1988   "England's Pleasant Land – Vision and reality"

1988   "Feast Amid Famine" – International Video

1991   "The Reform of the CAP" – White Paper

1993   "The Miracle of Agriculture" – Gold Award Video

2000-   Agricultural obituary writer for *The Times*

2006   An UnOrdinary Life

My early life with Anthony – The distaff view 1
Farming News 24th January 1996

A farmer's wife – me? Never. Not in my wildest dreams. In 1954 I was a town girl, a secretary in London and loving it. Out in the Sticks? Mud and wellie boots? No, certainly not.

But somehow I found myself standing at the alter promising to love, honour and obey the usual writer of this column who had that week left agricultural college. What a commitment! Anthony Rosen was, at that time, quite slim, cherub-faced and rather shy, all of which were to change rapidly.

With no farming experience whatsoever, other than school holidays spent on his Uncle's farm, Anthony took a job as head tractor driver (of two) on a farm in Gloucestershire. It was a rundown farm, poorly equipped, but an interesting experience nevertheless. The sheep were always "out" and the main crop seemed to be myxamatosed rabbits and horses: the blackberries in the hedgerows were as big as damsons.

We lived in a picturesque cottage in the middle of an orchard with neither electricity nor bathroom – only an outside loo. We traipsed up to the farmhouse each evening for a bath and were often waylaid by our employers as we emerged and invited us to have a drink. There we were, scrubbed, shining and clutching our damp towels while our employers, since they "dressed" for dinner every night, were in all their finery! Only newly-weds would have put up with it and one would not dream of offering such accommodation to a farm worker today, I am glad to say.

But I am grateful that I have trimmed the wick of a paraffin lamp, coped without a refrigerator and washed socks by hand. It was all part of my education. But I was nevertheless happy when, with a year's experience on his CV, Anthony set his sights higher and was offered a job as farm manager on a newly-purchased 200-acre farm in West Sussex.

The owner of the farm had made a great deal of money on the stock exchange, which he was happy to invest in agricultural land and farming. "You leave the stock-broking to me and I'll leave the farming to you" was Anthony's broad brief. And so it was.

Machinery was purchased, a dairy herd established and buildings erected, two massive reservoirs were dug for the organic irrigation system and the difficult weald clay was coaxed into producing some goodish cereals and spectacular grass. Neighbouring farms were purchased and the ultimate acreage became 1,650 acres, all tile-drained.

It was with trepidation that Anthony first showed me the house where we were to live for the departing tenants (bought out for £2,300) boasted that there hadn't been a woman in the house for nineteen years. I still remember the unspeakable smell coming from an old black pot bubbling on the ancient range, the holey socks hanging on a string in front of a smouldering fire and the grimy dining room table on which stood several messy sauce bottles – and a shaving mug, razor and mirror. The mind boggles.

The house had to be fumigated and then an army of builders moved in and quickly turned it into a really lovely home with every mod con possible which was just as well as our first-born ("I want to be a farmer") was about to put in an appearance, to be fairly quickly followed by his brother ("I will be a stockbroker first and a farmer second") – sensible child.

Since we were very "state of the art" with our herringbone parlour, 300 zero grazed cows, organic irrigation, large granary, and all modern equipment, many individuals and groups came to see us, to compliment, criticise or simply enjoy. And they all had to be fed. I well remember some children from a London grammar school who didn't like the thought of drinking milk that came from a cow, preferring "nice clean bottles".

Life was not perfect all the time. One morning we woke to find the entire dairy herd in our garden, a gate having been carelessly left open by a member of the hunt. My poor herbaceous border!

And there was the time when our bad-tempered bull broke a leading-chain while being handled and Anthony was thumped over a gate, badly dislocating his shoulder – ouch.

Another sad occasion was when we found three of our lovely young heifers dead in the field. The young Scots vet who came to do the post-mortems discovered that they had eaten mares' tails, a noxious weed. We were very impressed that while he worked he took time to explain the inner workings of these animals to two fascinated young boys – well beyond the call of duty, we thought.

This happy era came to an end after fifteen years when the owner's son was considered to be of suitable age to take over. Oh dear.

Anthony then thought hard and long. He had for some time believed that there was sufficient profit in farming to entice city institutions to invest in agriculture and eventually one large insurance broking company was persuaded that such an investment would be a good idea and thus Fountain Farming came into being.

Fountain Farming's first farm was purchased in 1971 in Hampshire, 1,040 glorious acres, each acre costing a then huge £312. The lovely farmhouse, of brick and flint, was to be our home.

I therefore found myself driving down to Hampshire in my Mini with our small daughter (6, "I want a pony"), our whippet, two cats, a rabbit and a muscovy duck – our sons were at school.

Anthony, having taken delivery of one of the first Range Rovers, arrived with a big smile and a more humdrum and less vociferous load.

And so started another chapter of our lives......

When I am asked, somewhat pityingly, by one of today's competent young career women, who juggle with jobs, husbands, nannies, homes and children "Were you just a housewife?" I smile to myself and reply "Yes, just a housewife...."

The controversy over Anthony Rosen rumbles on, so I thought this might be a timely moment to offer up the second part of my personal biography.

The first installment was about pre-Fountain Farming days and so this chapter starts with our life on the first Fountain Farming farm which was purchased in 1971 for £312 an acre. The farm, 1,040 acres of scenically beautiful top-quality chalk land in Hampshire, was exceptionally well equipped with two good houses, six cottages, and modern buildings, including a large dairy and new granary. The locals decided these "city-folk" were daft to be paying this sort of money for agricultural land: "£300 an acre – unbelievable!"

The large farmhouse was lovely, built of brick and flint, it overlooked the River Bourne, a lazy chalk stream well stocked with brown trout. The house, which became our home, had a large area at one end with a separate entrance, which served as Anthony's office and the headquarters of Fountain Farming.

One of the first jobs was to modernize the relatively new dairy buildings by installing the first Hosier rotary parlour to milk 220 cows. Simultaneously, dispersal sales were visited to purchase both cows and heifers.

Some Friesian heifers, supposedly maiden so as to minimize health risks, were purchased from a reputable dealer in Ireland. Seven of these "maidens" were subsequently found to be in calf. On complaining to the Irish dealer Anthony was asked what on earth was the matter since he had seven extra animals. So why worry?

Anthony spent a lot of time looking at other suitable farms to come under his umbrella, so an experienced manager was appointed to run the Hampshire farm, which with the addition of two nearby farms (£270 and £330 an acre) had grown to 1,750 acres.

Efficient secretaries manned the office, typing at the speed of light on their electric typewriters. Still plodding along on my manual machine I was, therefore, relegated to the back burner, or to be more accurate to the Aga.

There was a large throughput of people in the office – salesmen, advisors, candidates being interviewed for various jobs, journalists, potential investors and so on and they all seemed to find their way eventually into our large kitchen to be sustained with whatever food was around.

There was always coffee on the bubble and cakes in the tin and looking back this probably laid the foundation for Anthony's current battle with the bathroom scales.

We also had regular press lunches, because publicity – good publicity – was vital to attract both the best employees and more investors. We were one day almost embarrassed to hear that our press lunches had become famous in Fleet Street, the home of journalism at that time. What a pressure.

I remember one poor journalist who refused mouth watering home-grown roast lamb and all the delicious roast vegetables which went with it since he was a "cradle" vegetarian. This was quite unusual in those days and even more so since he was then the editor of Livestock farming. We all admired his good manners when he pronounced his mound of unadulterated sprouts "delicious".

Potential investors were sometimes taken to see prospective Fountain Farming properties by helicopter taking off from our walled garden. This was all very well in winter but one spring, with bulbs in full bloom, our daffodils were all neatly decapitated by the slipstream. From then on helicopters were banished to the adjoining field, necessitating a very short walk – oh dear.

We were one time asked to take part in a BBC's "Breakfast with......" programme. Anthony readily accepted but I was somewhat daunted. The programme was not to go out live but was recorded a day or two before but at breakfast time to give the right "feel". I dispatched our small daughter to school early. Prepared a large quantity of kedgeree, not knowing how many people I had to feed, and hoped for the best.

Three large BBC vehicles weighed down with technicians and equipment appropriated a nearby barn and moving around in my kitchen became a real hazard as wires trailed everywhere, sound recording equipment attached. We were temporarily taken over by the BBC.

In the event Anthony was, of course, very fluent (when is he not?). When asked by one of the two interviewers how recently he had actually milked a cow his prompt reply was "Probably at the same time as you, David (Richardson), last drove a tractor."

I was happily clinking the cups at suitable moments, when horror upon horror, Tony (Parkin's) question came my way. I had a sleepless night afterwards wondering if I had said something completely stupid, but when it was broadcast it transpired that my guardian angel must have been with me as it sounded almost all right.

Our daughter, who was at day school locally, had her own farming enterprise – twelve beady-eyed chickens, who frequently reconnoitered the kitchen, clucking companionably, bottle-fed lambs in season who thought they were whippets and ran to retrieve balls, whippets who grazed thinking they were lambs, a muscovy duck who was as good as any guard dog and various cats, rabbits and guinea pigs. I had, so far, managed to resist the demands for a pony but the local riding school had a very dedicated pupil.

Our two sons were away at school at this time but the moment they came home it was a case of boots on and out to see what was going on. They had their uses since both of them had learned to drive tractors and combines before the thirteen-year old age restriction came in and they were both competent and responsible.

They were once lured by the offer of £2 to beat for the visiting shoot. They set off cheerfully enough but two ashen figures returned at the end of the day and one was physically sick. Never again, they said. A good reaction I thought.

The children grew. Fountain Farming grew. And Anthony grew. Our lives continued, busy and satisfying.

Yes, Anthony is controversial, but boring – never.

APPENDIX – Milk Quotas

During the latter half of March 1984 the late Sir Stephen Roberts, then Chairman of the Milk Marketing Board, stated bluntly "Milk quotas will be imposed only over my dead body".

One week later, on Thursday, 31 March 1984, Michael Jopling, UK Minister of Agriculture, shattered the stunned dairy industry by announcing that he was accepting the recommendations of the European Community and as from 2 April, two days later, all British dairy farmers would have to cut their production by nine per cent.

Effectively this ensured that Britain could never be self-sufficient in milk products. In contrast to the lack of planning which had shattered our industry, both the Irish and Dutch governments ensured that their dairy farmers were provided with a much healthier quota. The Irish quota meant that Irish dairy farmers could produce 3187 pints per head of the population: the Dutch farmers 1600 pints: while the pitiful UK quota was pegged at 545 pints per head of the UK population. All these allowances were to be based on the previous two years production.

No thought whatsoever had gone into the huge number of injustices this hasty imposition would cause. What of the dairy farmer who had, or was in the process of, improving his dairy buildings, or even starting a new herd? The arguments went on for years.

Another underclass, of which I was one, was the tenant farmer - for to whom did the milk quota belong? Was it the landlord's or was it the tenant's? The government had not even considered such mundane matters. The Minister never did understand the difference between 'cut in output' and 'cut in profits'.

Indeed the ill-considered imposition of milk quotas has to rank alongside governments' appalling mishandling of both the BSE (Bovine Spongiform Encephalopathy) crisis and later the 2001 foot-and-mouth disaster which brought untold and unnecessary misery to a large number of farmers.

In 1989, I fortuitously met the MAFF Chief Vet in the Farmers' Club who assured me that I was making too much of the BSE crisis and that "in two years time BSE will be but a distant memory". BSE cases peaked in 1992 with more than 37,000 cases. There were 117 confirmed cases in 2005. But I have yet to be convinced that there is any relationship between BSE and human CJD (Creutzfeldt-Jakob Disease).

I had already agreed to return Hedge End Farm to the landlords, the Prudential, in September 1984 and the question of who owned the milk quota of 1.4 million litres became a hot topic. Indeed the Prudential, within twelve months of my departing sold the quota for which I received nothing for £440,000.

Two years later, in 1986, the government brought in an equitable scheme whereby the tenant and the landlord shared the value of the milk quota according to who had done what to earn the quota. In the case of Hedge End I would have qualified for 100 per cent of the value since during the eleven years I had tenanted the farm the Pru had invested nothing in the dairies. The 1986 Act was, sadly, not retrospective.

The milk quota battle became a *cause celebre* and I ended up representing, on a strictly honorary basis, eighty-nine tenants who had had some 35 million litres of quotas "stolen" by their landlords. Even the fact that Gordon Lee-Steere, then President of the Country Landowners Association, publicly insisted in 1985 on compensating an outgoing tenant with the full value of the quota, did nothing to mitigate the injustice.

Of the eighty-nine tenants one, a tenant of the Marquess of Cholmondeley, the Lord Great Chamberlain, was so impoverished that he qualified for legal aid, so we took his case to the High Court as a test case.

The hearing was a farce for, after hearing representations from lawyers acting for Denis Bostock and more lawyers representing the Marquess, the CLA and others, the judge returned immediately after the luncheon break with a four page typewritten judgement which had clearly had to have been written before he had even heard the case. However the judge allowed an appeal to the Appeal Court. Ironically on the day of the judgement the will of the Marquess was publicised – the biggest amount ever left....and poor Bostock was seeking only £15,000 in compensation.

On the 14 October 1991 seventeen lawyers, of whom one represented legally-aided Bostock sat before the three judges of the Appeal Court. One of the Cholmondeley lawyers suggested that since it was seven years since milk quotas had been imposed it would be grossly unfair if landlords now had to find money to compensate their tenants "for they may well have spent it". To say that the three judges fell about laughing would be no exaggeration: one responded "and if one of the landlords had had a particular good win with the money on the gee-gees would that mean he should pay more?"

The judges found unanimously in favour of Bostock and instructed that his case should be taken to the European Court of Justice. The legal-aid authority was extremely helpful and agreed to back his case. Unfortunately the case in Europe was heard at the same time as the negotiations for the Maastricht Treaty were being carried out. The Maastricht Treaty (formally, the Treaty on European Union) was due to be signed on 7 February 1992 in Maastricht, Netherlands between the members of the European Community and subsequently entered into force on 1 November 1993, under the Delors Commission. It led to the creation of the European Union and was the result of separate negotiations on monetary union and on political union.

The judges were certainly not going to jump into the political cauldron by ordering the British government to bring in a new law relating to events some nine years earlier so they decided that although "some landlords had certainly being unfairly enriched at the expense of their tenants it should be left to the British government to right this wrong". So we were back where we started and the Conservative government declined to even consider compensation.

Following the 1997 election and the massive victory of Labour I arranged to see the junior agriculture Minister, Lord Donahue. He was overtly extremely sympathetic but declined to take action to put right a wrong perpetrated by the previous government.

At that I called it a day: I wrote a personal letter to each of the eighty-nine disaffected tenants. Four wrote back and thanked me for the fourteen years of effort on their behalf.

1973

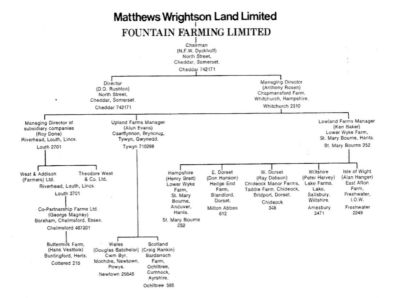

Matthews Wrightson Land Limited
FOUNTAIN FARMING LIMITED

The 75 Club

Even today with our enhanced systems of communication it is difficult for relatively isolated farmers to keep in touch with others. The pressure of the day-to-day running of a farm can lead to a sense of isolation: this was especially so in the 1950s and 1960s.

Thus it was that in March 1968 fellow farmers John Jenkins and Chris Ford and I suggested to a select few that we should form a small luncheon club, who would meet quarterly in London, inviting a guest to invigorate the discussions based on current agricultural problems.

Richard Ecroyd, Michael Worth, Frank Paton and Tony Keen, all substantial farmers, agreed to join: thus it was that on the 23rd April 1968 we met at The White House in London with Alan Mitchell, a leading UK agricultural banker as our guest.

Our first chairman, John Jenkins, even then a serious wine buff and later to develop a serious high quality wines business, ensured that we both drank and ate well.

A year later, ten members, Derek Pearce, Bill Green and Tim Denham Smith having joined, lunched HRH The Duke of Edinburgh who was at that time an impressive relatively young royal, the first royal visit of six: he commented very favourably on the sustenance we provided and presented us with a dynamic view of farming.

From then on it was relatively easy to attract important guests: for example every Minister of Agriculture lunched with us – until 1997.

We enrolled Hubert de Vriendt. an outstanding French farmer, (still a loyal member), Dutch farmer John Vlielander and David Mynett who farmed in Germany giving the Club a cosmopolitan feel.

During the next ten years we increased our membership to eighteen and they all attended the quarterly lunches which we then moved, via Quaglinos, to the Farmers Club on 8th April 1980 – but still bringing our own, Jenkins' inspired, wine! This venue, the Farmers' Club, provides excellent hospitality to this day.

By the mid 1990s time and fate had taken its toll with distinctly ageing Club members – no longer the dynamic young thrusting entrepreneurs of thirty years earlier. We had to decide whether it would continue until its last two remaining members handed in their mortal coil after a final lunch. Sense prevailed and a decision was made to invite some younger members to join us.

So by the time of our 150th meeting on 8th April 2003, at which the thriller author Frederick Forsyth was our guest, we had eighteen members, of which more than half could claim to be in the true tradition of the 75 Club, young thrusting entrepreneurs of the agricultural industry.

In addition to the quarterly meetings the Club occasionally takes a three day overseas tour: Germany, France and in 2007 it is planned to visit the Russian holdings of one of our members whose annual turnover exceeds £500 million!

Sadly one tradition of the Club, the placing of the four lunches a year as top of members' priorities, became more difficult to maintain and today with twenty-two members there is seldom more than an eighty per cent attendance. But to excuse this lapse it has to be admitted that the pressure on individual farmers today is far heavier than during the Golden Years of British Agriculture which effectively ended in 1986.

The Club certainly continues with its major objective of bringing together the leaders, and potential leaders, of the agricultural industry to meet and openly discuss matters that are, or could be, affecting the industry and thus their businesses.

Tuesday 23rd April 1968

Albany Room
The White House, Regents Park,
London N.W.1

Les Vins

Puligny Montrachet 1964

Château Haut Marbuzet 1964

Déjeuner

Terrine du Chef

Scampi Newburg

Poulet de Bresse Rôti au Romarin
Pommes Château
Endives Braisés

Tranche d'Ananas au Kirsch

Café

Mr Alan Mitchell

First 75 Club Menu

Tuesday, 8th April, 2003
The Farmers' Club, London S.W.1.
Eastwood Room ~ 150th Meeting

Luncheon

Grilled Smoked Haddock Fillet
Welsh Rarebit Topping
Tomato and Spring Onion Salad

Fillet of Scottish Beef Wellington
with a Truffle & Madeira Sauce
Fresh Seasonal Vegetables

British Cheese and Biscuits

Coffee and Chocolate Mints

Frederick Forsyth Esg.

The Wines

Côte du Rhône
Guigal (White) 2000

Clos du Marquis
Saint-Julien 1996

150th Luncheon

181

Agricultural Tours

Illinois	June 1984	Chile	January 1996
Texas & Okl	June 1987	South Africa	March 1996
Texas & Ok	November 1987	Ecuador	April 1996
South Africa	January 1988	E.Germ/Cz	July 1996
California	June 1988	New Zealand	November 1996
Venezuela	November 1988	Chile	January 1997
South Africa	January 1989	Australia	February 1997
New Zealand	February 1989	Ecuador	October 1997
Kenya	October 1989	Texas	February 1998
Australia	Nov/Dec 1989	DC-3USA	April 1998
South Africa	January 1990	Australia	October 1998
Zimbabwe	October 1990	Cuba/Pan (1st Myst)	Nov 1998
Australia	Oct/Nov 1990	Ecuador	December 1998
Thailand	January 1991	Texas(TH)	February 1999
New Zealand	February 1991	Australia (Fly)	September 1999
Arizona	May/June 1991	Costa Rica (2nd Myst)	Oct/N
South Africa	Oct/Nov 1991	Argentina	January 2000
Thailand	Jan/Feb 1992	Texas/Okl	June 2000
Texas	February 1992	Costa Rica	Oct/Nov 2000
East Germany	July 1992	Ecuador	Jan/Feb 2001
Chile	January 1993	Chile	Mar/Apr 2001
Australia	March 1993	Colorado	May/June 2001
California	October 1993	Argentina	November 2001
New Zealand	November 1993	New Zealand	Feb/Mar 2002
Antigua (SC)	December 1993	Argentine	Jul/Aug 2002
Chile	January 1994	Ecuador	Nov 2002
Thailand	February 1994	Australia	Jan 2003
Co/Wy	June 1994	Chile	Feb/Mar 2003
Australia	October 1994	Colorado	May/Jun 2003
Chile	November 1994	South Africa	Feb/Mar 2004
Ecuador	January 1995	Chile	Feb/Mar 2005
Arizona	March 1995	Okavango/SA	Oct 2005
British Col	May 1995	Baltic States	Sep 2006
Maine	October 1995		

Past Club Chairman **Anthony Rosen** *went to his first Oxford Farming Conference in 1957 and has been to every one since. This year, as the OFC celebrated its sixtieth anniversary, Anthony was there for the fiftieth successive time. He reminisces about the changes he has seen over the past 50 years.*

My 50 years of attending the Oxford Farming Conference

THE MID-FIFTIES were an eventful time for me, as a relative newcomer to agriculture.

When I became a farm manager in 1956, I asked Guildford MAFF what statutory forms had to be kept. The bemused official admitted that he had never before been asked such a question, and it transpired that the statutory form filling requirement was not too onerous, anyway. A farmer was required to fill in the Annual June Census, maintain an Animal Movements Register, and record acreages and sales of wheat.

Look back in envy you young farmers of today, as you struggle to comply with the massive amount of bumph emanating from DEFRA and their ilk.

Those were the days when the far-sighted Committee of The Farmers' Club maintained the tradition that there would always be a ratio of two farmers to each ancillary member wishing to join the Club. The strength of the Club today - of which I have been a proud member for 40 years - is, in my opinion, due to the continuation of that rule.

Sadly, the Oxford Farming Conference has failed to appreciate a similar need to maintain an adequate percentage of practising farmers, either as delegates or as members of the committee.

The first Oxford Farming Conference was held in 1936, although this year's, because of the Second World War, was its sixtieth. In spite of odd blips, it remains - at least in perception - the UK's leading farming conference. This is mainly because what happens on the stage, however excellent the speakers, is simply to provide a backdrop to meeting old friends and new, and, in today's jargon, "net-working".

The OFC has altered over the years, until recently succeeding in keeping pace with the changes in agriculture. Back in the golden days, when farming was fun, the OFC was run, from 1954 to 1980, by Mike Soper (duly honoured at this year's conference), closely supervised by a nine farmer committee, three retiring from the committee each year.

Indeed it was not until 1966 that I, in my youthful enthusiasm for progress (sic), proposed that leading machinery manufacturer Tim Wilder join the committee, the first non-farmer to be elected post-war. This year's committee, however, consisted of two farmers and seven 'ancillaries'... surely a sad reflection on who, it is believed, now runs the countryside?

Of the three non-farmers newly appointed this year, one has never even attended an OFC.

During Mike's fiefdom every delegate, even when numbers exceeded 1000, received, by return of post, a receipt for his booking, together with a hand-written badge and a welcoming note. Today, with the aid of modern technology, one hears absolutely nothing after booking until a few days before the conference, when one then receives a badge with minuscule printing and with information of use mainly to the organisers. Progress?

The themes of the conferences over the years have anticipated the hopes and worries of farmers. Back in the 1960s and 70s, no one from the NFU was ever to be seen anywhere near the conference. Indeed, MAFF personnel were actually forbidden to attend, in case their minds were sullied by contemporary thoughts. But many did attend, incognito.

Farmers either went to the OFC or dutifully attended the routinely dreary NFU Annual General Meetings usually held a week or so after the OFC. How very different to more recent years, when both politicians and NFU leaders now consider attendance at Oxford essential.

The first *golden era* of British Farming was the period from 1812 - when the ex-farm price of wheat was £28 a ton - until 1870. This price, incidentally, was not equalled until 1973, following our entry into the EEC.

When the second *golden era* ended in the in the mid-1980s, there was an instant change in the attitude of farmers to their now less certain future. The OFC changed, too, to reflect the fact that farmers could no longer operate in their own, relatively pleasant goldfish bowl.

The eleventh OFC, my first, was held in the Playhouse Theatre in January 1957 and had as its theme *Better Management – Lower Costs*. The 420 delegates heard speakers ranging from Frank Sykes and John Young to Richard Roadnight, all memorable farmers.

To pay the fee for me to attend this three-day conference (full board), the farm had to sell less than half a ton of wheat. To attend the 2006 OFC, one needed the receipts from the sale of seven tonnes!

As a result of the change from a truly farming conference to one that feels it needs to pander to the rather more expensive tastes of non-farmers, the number of farmers attending has dwindled rapidly. This year I would estimate that there were fewer than 50 actual farmers present, plus a further 20, sponsored, younger farmers.

The reputation of the OFC has enabled it to command the best speakers from both home and abroad. For example, in 1970 Dr Magnus Pyke gave one of the most outstanding theatrical performances ever seen at Oxford, speaking to the not especially attractive title *Advances in Food Technology*.

The earth shattering (and misguided) effect of UK entry to the EEC took no time to be reflected at Oxford, and 1973 brought a plethora of famous speakers: John Sainsbury, Henry Fell (yes, even then!), economist Ian Reid, banker Bob Bruce and Bob Den Engelse, to name but a few, talking on the Conference theme: *Change – Challenge*.

This was followed in 1974 by, in my opinion, the greatest performance ever at Oxford, by USDA Professor George Mehrens who delivered a masterpiece on *World Food Production and its Problems*.

During discussion, when asked about the performance of the British Government towards its farmers, he declined, as a foreign dignitary, to comment on another government's actions. But later, at the informal supper at Worcester College (years later to become The Oxtail Club, held under Chatham House Rules) he stated: "What I am about to say I will deny I ever said, and everyone will believe me because nobody would believe that I would ever be so stupid as to say it".

There followed a destructive summary of the British Government's ignorance of world trade, especially in agriculture. And, in those days, even such a delicious indiscretion was never leaked.

The first dinner speaker ever to receive foot-stamping, which went on to reach a crescendo, was Opposition Leader Harold Wilson in 1964. He drizzled on for 47 minutes (thus confounding even the most pessimistic punter in the speech-length sweepstake) with a truly dire performance.

Then, as the 1980s loomed, the all powerful influence of politicians, especially those from the EU, became more pronounced. The legacy of Tom Williams, the last Minister to justify his title as "farmers' friend", was finally at an end. This was marked at Oxford by a succession of dreary political

186

performances by several political leaders who shall remain nameless.

When the OFC was at its zenith there was firm intention to keep to a minimum the number of speakers, thus allowing ample time for discussion: the general guidance was 10 speakers over the two days. At this year's conference the first day boasted five speakers in the morning and an unbelievable seven participants, in a discussion panel, in the afternoon. I believe that the first day's programme illustrates, beyond doubt, one of the ways in which the OFC is going wrong.

Minister Lord Bach presented well the ill-thought schemes of government and was followed by an excellent presentation by NFU President Tim Bennett. Then, instead of a sensible discussion period, two more good, but somewhat irrelevant, papers on Brazil and China were squeezed in.

Next came a masterly presentation by American Alex Avery (standing in for his famous father, Dennis, absent through injury) on *Should Britain Still be Farmed?* His conclusion was definitely 'Yes'.

It was obvious to everyone but the committee that the three main morning speakers could, with time for discussion, have usefully held the platform for the full three hours.

As for wasted time, six important speakers, chaired by Sir Don Curry, took part in the afternoon's grossly overloaded discussion panel. It was an insult to them – and also to the delegates, who had so little time to express their views.

In 1957, nearly 90 per cent of the OFC delegates were farmers, compared with this year when fewer than 10 per cent were present. My feelings are, that unless the OFC committee accepts the need for the conference to respect its title – a *farming* conference - and attract more farmers to attend (and to serve on the committee) I will go down in history with the dubious distinction of being the only person ever to attend 50 consecutive OFCs.

After all, for how much longer will the consultants, the agents, the media, the bankers, and other necessary but peripheral ancillaries want to continue networking with each other?

I hope I am wrong.

The success of The Farmers' Club is due entirely to the input of all members supporting an exceptional staff. If the Club is to retain its unique style and flavour, I trust that it will learn from the sad decline of the OFC to appreciate that it is essential for a *farming* establishment to keep up its membership of genuine farmers.

THE TIMES
July 05, 2003

Howard Paterson
Dynamo who shook up agriculture in the southern hemisphere

HOWARD PATERSON was New Zealand's greatest entrepreneur of recent years, a visionary in the realms of agriculture, biotechnology and other businesses. He was also director of some hundred companies, ranging from egg production to mobile medical testing. No venture was too way-out for this lateral thinker to consider, and he was never inhibited by traditional methods. He realised, for instance, that there was no limit to the scale on which farming could be done, and that there were economies to be gained from larger and larger operations.

Howard Paterson was born in Dunedin, New Zealand, in 1952. After reading philosophy and phenomenology of religion at the University of Otago, he went into property development both locally and overseas, his interests soon ranging across New Zealand, Australia, Fiji and the United States.

In 1988, only two years after the chaotic ending of farming subsidies in New Zealand, he decided that agriculture was becoming an interesting and challenging field in which to be involved. Within a year he owned 7,000 milking cows, and he very quickly expanded this dairy operation into a public company with no fewer than 52,000 cows. Later he was to buy back a controlling stake in the business, and after selling many of the farms to the resident share-milkers, he kept about 25,000 cows in New Zealand and in Tasmania. With the considerable success of this company, Tasman Agriculture, his activities soon ranged across the entire farming spectrum.

The deer farming industry, for instance, seemed to him to be in need of modernisation, so he expanded a relatively small operation into a vast deer empire with more than 100,000 animals spread over nine farms. Similarly, once he decided that egg production was a field to be conquered, he set up a state-of-the-art egg unit which now produces more than one million eggs daily and supplies 35 per cent of New Zealand's requirements.

More recently he was involved in developing a large new wine-producing area along the Waitaki Valley, anticipating that in time it would produce fine pinot noir. He was also heavily involved in a far-reaching project to improve the production of fine sheep wools.

Besides agriculture, New Zealand's pharmaceutical industry benefited greatly from his business acumen. Among the numerous companies in which he was involved — and most of which he founded — are several leading neutraceutical producers, including a company producing a biological means of controlling the fungal disease Botrytis in grapes and other susceptible plants.

Paterson was also responsible, jointly, for founding and financing the recently formed A2 Milk Corporation, marketing milk which is free from the potentially damaging beta-casein A1 protein, and which is being promoted as helping to prevent diabetes, heart disease and even mental illnesses.

As well as owning many tens of thousands of agricultural acres, Howard Paterson never lost his enthusiasm for land development, with projects such as a new town and an employment park near Canterbury in New Zealand. He was also active in the tourist industry, owning hotels and luxury resorts.

Despite his wealth and success, Paterson remained a modest man, more often seen in jeans than a suit. He was greatly respected in the business community — named New Zealander of the Year by the *National Business Review* last year — but more importantly earned the devotion of those who worked with him.

He is survived by his wife, Lee, whom he married in 1989, and their two sons, as well as by a son from his first marriage.

Howard Paterson, farmer and businessman, was born on November 7, 1952. He died, apparently of a heart attack, on July 1, 2003, aged 50.

Farming and the Nation

1986

Presented to the Nation

by

Anthony Rosen

December 1986

The Reform of the
Common Agricultural Policy

1991

Presented to the Nation

by

Anthony Rosen

June 1991

APPENDIX: South Africa - a combined black & white solution?

Even after a five week visit to a country one cannot obtain a thorough insight into its problems. However, combined with the knowledge gained from my four years (1988-1991) of consultancy in Zimbabwe where the problems facing the white farmers were similar, I came away from South Africa in March with a firm conviction. White farmers have a choice: follow the way of their colleagues in Zimbabwe into chaos and bloodshed or integrate.

In Zimbabwe I advised the Mashonaland Development Foundation: a strictly non-political organisation - but with fourteen members of the Mugabe government on its board! Robert Mugabe was born in Kutama, Mashonaland: he was educated there and his sister, Sabina, was the local MP. The local Kutama church presented the villagers with 520 acres of formidable scrub. The villagers cleared it by hand. No white farmer was prepared to help by bringing a tractor in to disc it.

It was suggested to the Commercial Farmers' Union, representing the 4,500 white farmers who owned 80 per cent of the farmable land, that they should sponsor a black farm management training scheme. "Why? They would not understand how to farm" was the white reply.

On it being suggested that if they refused to accept the inevitable and be seen to help the blacks they would lose their land, the classic response was "The country will go bankrupt without us: they cannot afford to take our land".

To outsiders the consequence of this narrow economic vision was inevitable, although one cannot condone the barbaric way in which it has happened. There were some notable exceptions amongst the white farmers who did indeed considerably help black Zimbabweans but these were treated with contempt by their fellow white farmers and there were not enough to influence the political antipathy to the noticeably affluent whites.

So South African white farmers have to make the choice: do they continue to accept the murder of three white farmers every week (yes, more than 1,500 have been murdered by professional killers in the past ten years) and ignore the inevitable demand for parity with their black neighbours or do they integrate? Will they anticipate the inevitable and be seen to be positively working with their fellow black men?

On my travels I did meet three superb examples of this black empowerment encouraged by visionary whites: two in vineyards and one growing table grapes (see photo).

The owner of the largest South African table grape operations treated his workers as human beings and knew the name of every one of his workers, both in the fields and in his pack-houses (see photo) and provided a crèche. After singing for their visitors, one little girl ran forward, arms outstretched, to be picked-up by the boss (see photo). Their attitude to further integration was impressively positive.

As one who has visited this beautiful and productive country eight times since 1988 one can only pray that the white farmers there will learn from the disastrous example of their Zimbabwean colleagues and mitigate the worst effects of racist prejudice.

The agricultural consultant with extensive foreign experience ran a successful farming operation for many years but then made the classic mistake of thinking that performance was more important than personalities.

MY EARLY impressions of farm life were formed during the War years, when I spent frequent school holidays on my uncle's farm in Suffolk.

It seemed a near-idyllic life with long summer days spent turning ripening hay, stooking sheaves of corn and walking behind the horses, harrowing or rolling the heavy Suffolk soil. It never rained.

During National Service I was taught to fly by the Army, and from the air farming looked even more appealing – tranquil, scenic and prosperous.

And so, after a high-pressure one-year agricultural course, I gained some useful experience working, as a head tractor driver (of two!) on a farm in Gloucestershire. Managing a farm for a wealthy businessman came next, and there I initiated the development of an expanding farming operation.

But 15 interesting and happy years later, nepotism reared its ugly head – in hindsight fortuitously.

In the 1960s there were good returns to be made on capital invested in tenant farming, so in 1971 I put a proposition to an ex-Army flyer friend, who was then managing director of Matthews Wrightson, the influential insurance brokers.

With their strong support, and capital, Fountain Farming came into being, alongside Matthews Wrightson's already established Fountain Forestry.

By the mid-1970s, Fountain Farming had become the largest farming company in Europe with more than 30,000 acres. It grew cereals, vegetables and grass, and had 6,200 dairy cows, plus followers, 3,000 beef animals and 25,000 sheep. Annual turnover was more than £6million.

Running parallel to the British operation was an Iranian enterprise, called Sherkate Sahami Landkesht, which grew 6,000 acres of irrigated vegetables. At that time, the Shah was sitting firmly on his throne.

In 1978, there came two revolutions. The much-publicised one caused the abdication of the Shah of Iran and the end of our operations there – fortunately with no financial loss. The other, more discreet but more serious for me, was the dramatically orchestrated removal of the MW company chairman, my Army friend.

My biggest mistake was in believing that performance was more important than personality. It isn't.

I initially thought that the removal of the chairman meant simply that I would continue to run Fountain Farming from its rural fastness and could ignore the musical chairs at head office. How wrong I was.

It soon became apparent that the new team at Stewart Wrightson (as Matthews Wrightson had become) had decided that the "country boys" must go. I was summoned to head office.

There I was informed that Fountain Farming was to be sold and that I could have no more than three months, instead of the 18 months that I felt was necessary, to sort out the 46 agricultural tenancies and find a new owner.

Following a typical City decision, what had been a phenomenally profitable and expanding business, employing 200 people, was split up and the hard-won land returned to its landlords. Many of these landlords are farming the land today, in all cases highly profitably.

'My Second Biggest Mistake'

Anthony Rosen

'The agricultural consultant who did not learn from 'His Biggest Mistake'

In 1988 I was approached by Howard Paterson, a young, then 35 years old, New Zealander who had amassed a considerable sum of money from property development in both his own country and elsewhere. He contacted me with a view to setting up a large-scale New Zealand type sheep operation in the United Kingdom.

After three days showing him the least unsuitable parts of England and Scotland I was easily able to convince him that such an enterprise could never be an economic success, particularly in view of the excessive land prices.

However he was determined that he wanted to do "something in agriculture". I asked him whether he had considered dairy farming in his home country, especially in South Island, where every resource necessary was absurdly cheap following the remarkable overnight removal of practically all farm subsidies.

In 1985 the Federated Farmers of New Zealand had taken the progressive decision to suggest to government that neither the country nor the farming industry could afford to continue with a system of support which contributed some 40 per cent of the New Zealand farmers' incomes: a system which destroyed the economic initiative of farmers and left them brain damaged, little different to drug addicts waiting for their next fix. Not surprisingly the government responded willingly and, showing no mercy, ended support, effectively overnight. Of 30,000 farmers some 800 went out of business, but all with enough money to buy a house. The most dramatic effect was that every resource necessary to farm dropped by 75 per cent. Thus it was possible to buy good agricultural land in South Island for under £100 an acre and a good down-calving cow was even cheaper.

We discussed the likely profitability of a 1,000 head dairy unit near his home town of Dunedin. One year later Howard Paterson was milking 7,200 cows: the land, the cows and the brand-new dairy units had cost him exactly £242 per cow place. Being a rare lateral thinker he had decided that if one thousand cows would be profitable then seven thousand would be even better. After further on-site discussions he expanded to 17,000 cows and placed the whole operation on the NZ share market, the business growing successfully to 52,000 cows.

Not content with this, and being unencumbered by family farming tradition, he went in to both large-scale egg production and deer farming. In addition his contribution to other aspects of New Zealand business life had led him to initiate and participate in many other national ventures, both in agriculture and allied fields. This earned him the coveted title of "Businessman of the Year".

In 2000 he was persuaded by a progressive scientist, Dr Corran McLachlan, that there were considerable differences in the composition of cows' milk, Corrie's theory being that milk containing only the A2 beta-casein was considerably healthier in its whole milk form than that containing the A1 beta-casein. The proportion depended largely on the breed of the cow with the Guernsey breed being the best and Ayrshires being the worst. I quickly became heavily involved in this fascinating concept, giving up all my other interests to concentrate on spreading the "A2 gospel".

Then just three years later double disaster struck, both Paterson and McLachlan died: Paterson, aged fifty from sleep apnoea and McLachlan, aged fifty-nine, from a most rapid cancer.

On Paterson's untimely sudden death, aged fifty, his chicken units were producing one million eggs a day and his deer farms comprised about 100,000 head. In all Paterson's many businesses employed more than one thousand people. I, thinking that the A2 directors would wish to continue the dreams of Paterson and McLachan, went on spreading the A2 gospel.

Sadly this was not to be, since the remaining board members appeared to have little interest in furthering the medical claims of A2 and were mainly interested in preserving their jobs and salaries. The share price of A2 collapsed and A2 patents were violated throughout the world with no apparent objection from the A2 company executives.

Three months after the deaths, I having regularly submitted, as previously, uncontested monthly consultancy accounts A2 suddenly decided that I had already been sacked, three months prior to the deaths of Paterson and McLachlan. I sued them for the three months of fees due before the deaths and the three months after. The case was due to be heard, eighteen months later on April 18th 2005 in Dunedin. I was booked to leave my house at 8.00am on the previous Wednesday to fly out to New Zealand to contest the case, but I was woken at 5.25am – not a good time of the day to be making important decisions - to be told that A2 had offered to settle my account up to the deaths but not after. I was facing a twenty-four flight, considerable personal expenses and a court bill, in all, more than £20,000, this to try and recover £12,000 fees plus part of my overall legal expenses if I did not accept their offer. The New Zealand "justice" (sic) system is different to the UK's in that one cannot recover more than two thirds of one's legal costs however clearly one wins the case.

To my eternal regret I accepted their offer thus missing the opportunity to demonstrate in court how the current A2 executives care nothing for furthering the aspirations of Paterson and McLachlan for A2 milk to make a significant contribution to world health.

I remain completely confident that A2 milk will, one day, make a dramatic change in world health, especially in the fields of diabetes and childhood allergies, but certainly not while its future is under the control of the present uninspired incompetents in New Zealand.

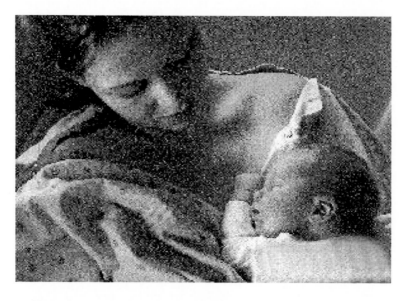

The latest addition to the Rosen clan, great-grandson
Evan Thomas – born to Melanie on 7th December 2006